Sorrow might come in the end

Legal cases in the music and entertainment industries

Jeremy Grice

Jeremy Grice

DEDICATION

To Sarah, Mathew, Rebecca and Rachel Grice

ACKNOWLEDGMENTS

Thank you to my colleagues at Liverpool Institute for Performing Arts for their support in undertaking this project. In particular, thanks go to Dawn Bebb and Harry Roberts for proof-reading every case study, to Maria Barrett for constant advice and guidance, and to Rachel Grice for the *Sources of Income* diagram in the Spandau Ballet case.

ISBN-10: 1491065745

ISBN-13: 978-1491065747

ABOUT THE AUTHOR

Jeremy Grice is Head of the Music, Theatre and Entertainment
Management degree at Liverpool Institute for Performing Arts,
where he teaches Financial Management and Entertainment Law.
He has a BA (Hons) in Hispanic Studies from Liverpool
University, an MBA from Durham University Business School,
and an LLM in Business and Commercial Law from Liverpool
John Moores University.

CONTENTS

Jeremy Grice

INTRODUCTION

Sorrow will come in the end was the title of a song written in 1997 by Steven Morrissey, following his defeat in the UK Court in *Joyce v Morrissey*.[1] Its angry lyrics appeared to offer a message to his victorious opponent:

> *You pleaded and squealed and you think you've won*
> *But sorrow will come to you in the end.*

It finished somewhat chillingly:

> *A man who slits throats has time on his hands and I'm gonna get*
> *you, So don't close your eyes, don't ever close your eyes.*

Unsurprisingly, Morrissey's record label, Island Records, withdrew the track from the album before distribution.

Not every court case in the music, theatre and entertainment industry ends in such vitriol and not every participant appears as bitter after losing. Sometimes the combatants even work together again. But there are always lessons to be learned. Some disputes are settled before a case reaches court; the settlements may reflect the legal merits of the different sides, or may be a reflection of the financial muscle and/or bravado of the different sides. However, this book explores UK cases which actually reached court before being resolved; it examines the primary source of court transcripts, explains the background to the cases and analyses the judgment, highlighting the legal principles which were under examination. It evaluates the impact of the cases for the music and entertainment industries, and discusses what can be learned.

Jeremy Grice

RESTRAINT OF TRADE AND UNFAIR CONTRACTS

THE STONE ROSES

Following a fairly long gestation period, involving different line-ups and names, the Stone Roses recorded their first demo in August 1984, and played their first gig under that name in October of the same year. The line-up included three of the four band members who would eventually release their first album, *The Stone Roses*, some five years later.

The band always had an "*edgy*" approach. They appeared to be at odds with many of the key movers in the music industry in Manchester, such as Factory Records, and the Hacienda. An illustration of this was seen in 1985, when, frustrated by the perceived lack of attention the band were getting in Manchester, lead singer Ian Brown and drummer Alan Wren undertook a graffiti marketing campaign, spraying the band's name wherever they could in the city, including over some high-profile monuments. On another occasion, in 1988, they were booked to play a concert in Manchester, supporting James. However, they put up their own posters around the city, listing *themselves* as headliners, and changing their starting time in order to limit the time James could play.

In 1989, they were appearing on the Late Show, on the BBC. However, one minute into their performance the power failed, resulting in Ian Brown repeatedly yelling abuse at the presenter. The band was also not short of confidence, or some might say arrogance.

After their first album reached the charts in 1989, Ian Brown commented in NME:

> We're the most important group in the world, because we've got the best songs and we haven't even begun to show our potential yet.

It had taken them five years to reach this position. From 1984 the band were managed by Howard Jones, who had previously managed the Hacienda club. However in 1986 he left to concentrate on managing on the Thin Line record label, which he had set up originally to release the Stone Roses' album.

At the time, a businessman named Gareth Evans, who had originally made his money in the world of hairdressing, was looking to get involved in the growing Manchester music industry. He had already set up a venue called the International as a rival to the Hacienda. He then advertised in the newspaper for bands to manage and when the Stone Roses approached him, he agreed to be the band's manager, following a slightly surreal first meeting during which Evans apparently dropped his trousers to show the band some underpants he had been distributing (for full details see the 2004 BBC3 documentary: *Blood on the Turntable*).[2]

The deal which was agreed with Evans gave him 33% of the band's earnings for 10 years; both figures were unusually high for management deals in the music industry. One member of the band, Andy Couzens, refused to sign it. This eventually led to Couzens' departure, with Evans allegedly engineering a split between him and the other band members. The remaining members of the band signed the management contract with Evans in December 1986.

In June 1987, bass player Pete Garner left, eventually replaced by an old schoolfriend of the other band members, Gary "Mani" Mountfield.

His recruitment made a huge difference to the band's sound, with Ian Brown commenting:

When Mani joined it almost changed overnight [...] Straight away, everything just fell into place.[3]

Gareth Evans set up a rather surprising record deal with FM Revolver, a record company that focused on heavy metal. They established the Black Records label specifically for the Stone Roses, and recorded and released the single "*Sally Cinnamon*", which, whilst selling all 1000 copies which were produced, made no real impact. Evans claimed that FM Revolver were not interested in promoting the Stone Roses, and went to look for an alternative label. His second choice of company was also surprising to many. He was attracted by the roster of Jive Records, part of the Zomba Music Group. However, Jive had a reputation for agreeing contracts which were heavily weighted in their favour, as James Ware, Music Industry lawyer, highlighted during the *Blood on the Turntable* documentary:

The problem with Jive as a record company was that its contracts were notorious in the industry, and for myself, and for most of my colleagues, I wouldn't recommend an artist to sign it.

Nevertheless, the band signed to Zomba, and was assigned to the newly formed Silvertone Records. Silvertone released the band's first album, *The Stone Roses*, in April 1989. It reached number 19 in the UK Album charts, and led to a number of successful UK chart singles. In 1990 the band won four NME Readers polls. They performed to over 27,000 people at an outdoor concert at Spike Island in Widnes, although the concert suffered from substantial sound and organisational problems. In July 1990, the single "*One Love*" was released and reached number four in the charts. It turned out to be the band's last release for Silvertone.

The band's success led FM Revolver to re-release *Sally Cinnamon*, accompanied by a video. The band disliked the video intensely, and showed their "edgy" side in their response. On their way to a gig in South Wales, they called in at FM Revolver's office in Wolverhampton, having previously stopped off at a FADS paint store. They attacked the offices, and the cars parked outside, with paint. The following day they were arrested, and ended up in court where they were each fined £3,000.

The band had entered into two agreements with Zomba in April 1988. The first was a *recording* agreement, made originally between Zomba Productions Limited and the four band members. The agreement was then assigned to Silvertone Records Limited. The second agreement was a *publishing* agreement, made between Zomba Music Publishers Limited and the band members.

By 1990, the band was unhappy with Zomba and Silvertone, and wanted to extract themselves from the agreements. There were unsuccessful attempts at renegotiation amid suggestions from Gareth Evans that the agreements were unfair and a restraint of trade, and therefore unenforceable. In September 1990, Silvertone and Zomba placed an injunction on the band to stop them recording with another label. They then instigated court proceedings against the band members and their manager to confirm that the contracts were valid and enforceable. The date of the court case was initially set for November 1991, however it was brought forward after the band complained that this would sideline them for over a year. The case was heard in March and April 1991, before His Honour Judge Humphries, who gave his judgment on 20 May 1991.

Precedents

There were a couple of precedents which were of particular relevance to the claims made by the Stone Roses.

In 1974 a young songwriter named Tony Macaulay won a case against his publisher, with whom he had entered an exclusive services agreement. The agreement was for an initial five-year period, with an automatic extension for a further five years if total royalties in the period exceeded £5,000. However, the publisher could give one month's written notice. The songwriter was successful in claiming that the contract was an unreasonable restraint of trade and therefore void. The court felt that there was a lack of obligation for the publishers to do anything with the writer's material, and that there should have been options for the songwriter to terminate the agreement.[4]

In 1988 a recording company, and its sister publishing company called Perfect Songs, took action against Holly Johnson when he wanted to leave the band, Frankie Goes to Hollywood. They claimed that he could not sign a contract with another recording or publishing company, as he was tied to them by a *"leaving member"* clause in the band's contract with them. Holly Johnson successfully claimed that the agreements were one-sided and unfair, and therefore unenforceable. The initial court judgment of February 1988 was confirmed in the Court of Appeal in July 1989. The court was persuaded that the contracts were unfair first because of how long they could potentially last when option periods were included; secondly, by the fact that the band members had no option to get out of the contract; and thirdly because of the power that the company had over the decision whether or not to release the band's recordings.[5]

Judge Humphries' decision

Judge Humphries began his analysis by confirming his appreciation of the financial risk which record companies take in investing in up-and-coming groups, and by accepting their need and right to protect their interests:

*What no company wants is to spend money, time and effort on
assisting a budding group up the ladder and then to have it plucked
from their hands when the group blooms.* [6]

He recognised that the relationship between the plaintiffs and the
defendants had been one of mutual benefit:

*The Stone Roses have in fact benefited considerably from the
promotion activities of the Zomba Group, and the Zomba Group
have benefited financially from the success of the Stone Roses.*

The Judge then highlighted a number of important factors in
relation to the negotiation and agreement of the contracts between
the Stone Roses and Zomba:

- Zomba were keen to tie up a deal with the Stone Roses as
  they were aware of interest from another, well-respected,
  independent record label, Rough Trade.

- At an initial meeting in March 1988 in Manchester, at which
  broad terms were agreed, it was made clear that, whilst
  there were separate recording and publishing agreements,
  the signing of one depended on also signing the other.

- At a further meeting in London on 10 April 1988 the only
  query raised by the Stone Roses' representatives was a
  request for higher royalties (which was refused). Zomba's
  representatives were surprised that no negotiation took
  place regarding a number of issues they saw as important
  and contentious.

- Senior executives at Zomba subsequently expressed concern
  at the lack of negotiation, questioning whether this might
  make the contract unenforceable.

- The contract was formally signed by all parties by 12 April 1988.

Having set the context, Judge Humphries examined each of the two contracts in turn, first to determine whether the contract should be considered to be "*restraint of trade*", and then to determine, if that were the case, whether such restraint was reasonable or unreasonable.

The Recording Contract

Judge Humphries commenced his examination of the Recording Contract by stating:

It is clear that not every agreement to render services exclusively to another is automatically within the restraint of trade doctrine.

He quoted Lord Reid from the case involving Tony Macaulay:

Any contract by which a person engages to give his exclusive services to another for a period necessarily involves extensive restriction during that period of the common law right to exercise any lawful activity he chooses in such manner as he thinks best. Normally the doctrine of restraint of trade has no application to such restrictions: they require no justification. But if contractual restrictions appear to be unnecessary or to be reasonably capable of enforcement in an oppressive manner, then they must be justified before they can be enforced.[7]

The recording contract between Zomba and the Stone Roses bound the Stone Roses not to record any of the musical works for a period of ten years after the contract expired. It also gave Zomba:

the irrevocable sole and exclusive right and license whether now in being or hereinafter arising throughout the Territory to use and

> *exploit the Masters in perpetuity and may exercise such rights or*
> *refrain therefrom as Zomba shall deem*

As a result of the above restrictions, Judge Humphries determined that the recording contract was restraint of trade, observing:

> *I have no doubt that the contract allowed the plaintiffs to prevent*
> *the Stone Roses from pursuing their primary means of output of*
> *their talents - making records and the like - for many years.*

He then considered whether, notwithstanding the restraint of trade, the contract was unlawful or not. The first area he examined was the balance of expertise between the parties when the contract was negotiated. On the one side, the representatives of Zomba had substantial expertise in the music industry, and were supported by lawyers who were well-established in the music industry. They also had considerable financial resources. On the other side, the Stone Roses were short of experience and short of money. Their manager, Gareth Evans, had some financial resources, and some business experience, though not, the Judge suggested, as much as he claimed to have. The Judge described him as enthusiastic and a *"plausible, excitable character"*, but also observed that he was *"entirely unversed in contractual law and in particular in the sort of contract which was in April 1988 being considered."* Evans and the band were supported by a solicitor, Mr Geoffrey Howard, but he also lacked any experience in the music industry.

Judge Humphries emphasised the importance of using lawyers who are experienced in the music industry when agreeing contracts of this nature:

> *They need the expertise to appreciate many of the terms, something*
> *of the state of the market, the state of the law on restraint and*
> *entertainment contracts, which in recent years has been developing*
> *rapidly. Music lawyers habitually get involved in negotiations and*

*know where it is right to and where they are able to put pressure on
the other side so as to thrash out an agreement which is fair to both
sides.*

A further concern for the Judge was the lack of evidence that the
contract had been genuinely negotiated between the parties. To
offset this, Zomba's representatives highlighted how they had
agreed in the initial meeting to pay a higher rate than originally
offered. However, this was counteracted by the lack of discussion
of other points, something that was admitted by their head of
legal and business affairs:

*Mr Furman was asked in the course of his evidence about non-
money matters being raised during negotiations but could not
remember any. He thought it odd that no query or negotiations on a
number of important matters arose and would have been prepared
to negotiate to the Stone Roses' advantage if there had been any
pressure from the other side.*

Having established that the expertise and negotiating position of
the parties were unbalanced, and that no real negotiation took
place, the Judge observed that such factors did not automatically
lead to the agreement being unfair:

*It is, however, possible even if one person has superior knowledge
and bargaining power for a fair agreement to be reached. Not
everyone who was in a position to do so misuses his power to take
advantage of the weaker party. I therefore propose to consider
whether in fact at the time of the contract the contract was fair.*

The contract provided Zomba with the *"irrevocable, sole and
exclusive right to the territory, to use and exploit the Stone Roses'
recordings"*. The territory was the *"world and its solar system"*.
However, what really disadvantaged the Stone Roses was that
Zomba had no obligation to do anything with the recordings,
even though they had exclusive control of them.

15

Judge Humphries observed that such terms might be justifiable if the duration of the contract were short or moderate. However, the minimum duration of the agreement itself, with the options open to Zomba, was at least seven years. It also contained a clause, which stated that options expired nine months following the release in the USA of a minimum number of records. There was no obligation on Zomba to release any recordings in the USA. Effectively, this meant that Zomba could extend the length of the agreement indefinitely by avoiding releasing records in the USA.

Zomba's representatives argued that the reference to the USA was a simple administrative mistake, and that it should have said "UK." However the Judge refused to accept that argument, observing that the words were clear and unambiguous, and whilst Zomba might not have intended to extend the agreement indefinitely, they were entitled to assign the agreement, and an assignee might have different intentions.

In many ways, the question of whether the USA reference was intended or not was irrelevant, as the agreement could in any event be extended for seven years, and the Judge felt that "*that even a seven-year sterilisation would be entirely unreasonable to young artists such as the Stone Roses were in May 1988.*"

He further supported this judgment by listing a number of clauses within the contract which he felt were unfair:

- A clause allowing Zomba the right to agree product endorsements without artist approval.

- A clause allowing Zomba the right to terminate the agreement on payment of a maximum of £1,500 to the Stone Roses, but with no termination right for the Stone Roses.

- A clause allowing Zomba to with-hold advances to the Stone Roses as result of ANY breach of the agreement, however minor.

- A clause providing Zomba with artistic control over recordings.

- A clause giving Zomba unlimited rights to assign the agreement elsewhere, without consultation with, or approval by, the Stone Roses.

- An expert witness, Mr Stinson, described the agreement as *"probably the most complete collection of nasty clauses [...] ever seen"*.

Judge Humphries concluded:

> *The contract with the terms I have discussed above incorporated is to my mind so entirely one-sided and unfair that no competently advised artist in the position of the Stone Roses would ever have agreed to sign it. I find affirmatively the contract was an unfair restraint of trade, has not been justified and is unenforceable.*

Zomba made one final attempt at rescuing the validity of the recording contract, by pointing to a clause in the contract relating to *"severance."* The clause stated that if any part of the agreement was to be found unenforceable then that part of the agreement would *"severed"* from the rest of the agreement, so that the rest of the agreement was still enforceable. Judge Humphries rejected the argument however, first on the grounds that he had found the whole agreement objectionable, not just some parts of it, and secondly because he did not accept that it would be reasonable for a party to use such a clause to change an unenforceable agreement into an enforceable agreement.

Publishing Agreement

Having examined the recording agreement in depth and detail, the Judge appeared not to feel the need to do the same with the Publishing Agreement. Nevertheless, he concluded that it had also not been negotiated fairly, due to the lack of legal advice and pressures which the Stone Roses were under. He further outlined other problems which he saw with the Publishing Agreement:

- It provided an irrevocable, exclusive assignment of all rights and copyrights in the compositions to Zomba, but they had only limited obligations to exploit the rights.

- The duration of the initial term of the contract was the same as the recording period; given the conclusion in relation to the recording agreement, then this could also be indefinite.

- The payment arrangements were "quite out of phase with normal and reasonable such agreements."

- The right of Zomba to over-ride the writer's artistic control was "*wider than is reasonable.*"

- He also concluded that, given the fact that all parties were aware that the recording contract and publishing contract were dependent on each other, the publishing contract should automatically be declared unenforceable once that decision had been made relating to the recording contract.

Aftermath

Following the case, the Stone Roses signed with Geffen Records, receiving a £2m advance. According to Gareth Evans, Geffen had already contributed £300,000 towards the legal costs in extracting themselves from the Silvertone contract.

One of the strategies used by Silvertone's representatives during the court case was to attempt to denigrate Gareth Evans, and to drive a wedge between him and the band. They highlighted the fact that he was taking commission of 33%, far higher than industry norm. More importantly, they revealed that in 1990 Silvertone had made a payment to the band (via Evans) of a Christmas "*bonus*" of £40,000. The band were furious as they were unaware that this amount had been received, as Evans had not mentioned it to them, claiming that he was retaining it to cover the legal costs relating to the contract. The rift festered, and not long after the successful court case the band sacked Evans as their manager. He sued them for breach of contract claiming £120,000 plus compensation. The dispute was settled out of court. During the *Blood on the Turntable* documentary, Evans claimed not to remember whether the settlement was £100,000 or £2m. He also claimed in the documentary that he was always aware that the contract would be unenforceable:

> *I knew that it was a bad contract. I knew what I was doing. I knew that contract would never stand up in court. That's why I signed it. I read it. That contract was tantamount to slavery.*

Other commentators in the documentary were of a different opinion. For example, music lawyer, James Ware remarked:

> *I can't conceive that a manager would deliberately sign a bad deal on the basis that that would give him the ability to get out of the deal later.*

Certainly, Evans' comments need to be taken with a pinch of salt. Throughout the documentary his view of his influence and importance in the Stone Roses' success was at odds with many of the other participants. Judge Jeffries also expressed the view that he was not a wholly reliable individual, commenting in his judgment:

Mr Evans was and is a plausible, excitable character, and had great shrewdness when it came to discussing money terms which he could understand. His plausibility leads him to exaggerate, often to speak without thinking. It is probably convenient to record at this stage I would rarely feel confident in acting on the evidence of Mr Evans if it did not fit in with his character as I have assessed it, or if it were not corroborated by other witnesses or other circumstantial evidence.

The band's second album was delayed due to family responsibilities and other personal issues within the band. They also moved away from their roots in Manchester, and spent a lot of time travelling around Europe. The album, modestly entitled *The Second Coming*, was finally released in December 1994. It sold well but received mixed reviews. In March 1995, drummer Alan "Reni" Wren left the band, and the planned appearance at Glastonbury a few months later was cancelled. They undertook a sell-out UK tour in the winter of 1995, however John Squire left the band in April 1996, and subsequent performances at Benicasim and Reading were disastrous, being heavily criticised for off-key delivery. A few months later the band disbanded.

Despite rumours, the band consistently and repeatedly denied that they would reform. In an article in Q Magazine in 2005, guitarist John Squire referred to Ian Brown as *"at best a tuneless knob and at worst a paranoid mess."* In 2011 Mani took exception to rumours arising after band members met at his mother's funeral, commenting to the NME:

Two old friends meeting up after 15 years to pay their respects to my mother does not constitute the reformation of the Stone Roses. Please fuck off and leave it alone. It isn't true and isn't happening.

However, in 2012 the band got back together and undertook a sell-out tour.

Subsequent cases

Courts are generally reluctant to interfere with contracts, which have been agreed between parties. This principle was laid out clearly by Lord Reid in 1968:

in general unless a contract is vitiated by duress, fraud or mistake, its terms will be enforced though unreasonable or even harsh and unconscionable... in the ordinary case the court will not remake a contract. [8]

Nevertheless, in the case of Silvertone and the Stone Roses, as in the preceding cases of *Schroeder v Macaulay* and *ZTT v Johnson*, the court was prepared to over-rule a contract which it believed was restraint of trade and unfair.

In 1994, another high profile case took place. George Michael claimed that the recording agreement he signed with Sony in 1988 was void or unenforceable on the grounds that it was unreasonable restraint of trade, and contrary to Article 85 of the Treaty of Rome. The agreement itself was a renegotiation of previous agreements which Michael had with the company. The Judge did not accept his claim, ruling that the Agreement was a compromise which had been renegotiated in good faith by the parties; that Michael was receiving benefits consistent with the obligations he had; that he had confirmed his acceptance of the Agreement by requesting an advance; and that the agreement was fair and necessary, in order to protect Sony's legitimate interests.

A further case occurred in 2000 when Shaun Ryder, formerly of the Happy Mondays and Black Grape, claimed that his agreement with the management of Black Grape was unreasonable restraint of trade, and had been obtained through undue influence. Ryder lost the case and a subsequent appeal.[9] The Court did accept that the agreement was unreasonable restraint of trade, and that there was undue influence. However, it ruled that Ryder's solicitor, and by association Ryder himself, had acted as if the agreement was valid, for example relying on some of the terms when a dispute occurred, even though they had always considered it to be invalid. The case demonstrated that when there is evidence that an artist and/or their representative act as if they believe a contract to be valid, even though they think it is unenforceable, then they will find it difficult or impossible to claim at a later stage that it is not enforceable.

The above cases highlight the importance of ensuring that inexperienced parties are provided with good advice prior to signing a contract, and standard clauses in music industry contracts will often ask artists to confirm that advice has been taken from a lawyer experienced in the music industry. Sometimes, a record company or artist manager will advance funds to a band to pay for this independent advice.

Andrew Evans, in his article *The Doctrine of Restraint in Relation to Music Industry Agreements*, concluded:

> *The music industry has taken a number of pragmatic responses to cases dealing with issues of control and there are emerging signs of increased "transparency" whilst acknowledging the "employer" holds the upper hand which makes sound financial sense to keep the artist happy. This has translated into an openness about contractual negotiation and terms that may pay long term dividends by fostering a closer and more trusting relationship between the parties.* [10]

LEGAL STRUCTURES AND INCOME SHARING

THE SMITHS

The Smiths were formed in Manchester 1982. The band initially came about as result of a meeting between Steven Patrick Morrissey and Johnny Marr. They later recruited Andy Rourke as bass player and Mike Joyce as drummer. The band finally broke up in 1987. During their time together they released a relatively small amount of original material: four core studio albums and 11 non-album singles. However they also produced a host of compilations and repackaged releases, both during their time together and in the years following. Despite the limited number of releases, the Smiths remain an iconic, influential and well-respected band in the indie UK music sector.

It is fair to say that life within the Smiths was never easy. Morrissey was a controversial character who made public pronouncements on a range of matters including politics and vegetarianism. The content of their songs, covering sensitive subjects such as the Moors Murders, also led them into difficulties at times. Johnny Marr suffered a long illness and at one stage was apparently on the edge of alcoholism. There was a protracted dispute with Rough Trade, their record label, which delayed the release of *The Queen is Dead*. Andy Rourke had a substantial heroin habit, which at one stage led the band to allegedly sacking him. At the time Morrissey was said to have left a post-it note on Rourke's car stating *"Andy – you have left The Smiths. Goodbye and good luck, Morrissey."* Whether the incident ever happened it still a matter of debate: Morrissey continues to deny it and Rourke continues to claim it occurred.[11] Morrissey's strong character certainly led him to dictate behaviour within the band. He was the staunch vegetarian but none of the other members were allowed to be photographed eating meat. A European Tour was abandoned at immigration when he decided that he didn't want to go.

The band broke up in 1987 after Johnny Marr, exhausted by the constant disputes and difficulties, took a two week break, during which a story was printed in the NME stating that he had left the band. He assumed the story had been planted by Morrissey, and decided to leave on his return from the break. He commented later that even *"signing on"* would have been better than remaining with the band. Following the breakup Johnny Marr participated in a range of bands and collaborations and Morrissey created a fairly successful solo career, still touring today. Joyce and Rourke have done little of note.

All the Smiths' songs were written in collaboration between Johnny Marr and Morrissey and accordingly they were jointly entitled to all song-writing and publishing royalties. For the most part, Marr and Morrissey also acted as the band's *"de facto"* managers. Managers came and went, fired by Johnny Marr at Morrissey's demand. Others who worked with the band were also dismissed at Morrissey's request, particularly if they became too close to Johnny Marr.

In an interview in Melody Maker in 1997, following the court cases, Morrissey provided his own perspective of the band dynamics, in comparing it to the court case proceedings:

> *Mike, talking constantly and saying nothing. Andy, unable to remember his own name. Johnny, trying to please everyone and consequently pleasing no one. And Morrissey under the scorching spotlight in the dock.*

Plenty has been written giving details of the history of The Smiths. In particular I would recommend *Morrissey and Marr: The Severed Alliance* by Johnny Rogan (Omnibus: 1992) and the *Light That*

Never Goes Out: The Enduring Saga of the Smiths by Tony Fletcher (Heinemann: 2012). There are also a number of TV documentaries, such as *These Things Take Time (Granada TV: 2002)* and *The Rise and Fall of the Smiths (BBC: 1999)*

An ongoing dispute over the distribution of profits from live performances and recordings was the cause of the legal case between Mike Joyce and Morrissey/Marr, which eventually reached the UK courts in 1996.

Mike Joyce's case

The case issued in March 1989 by Mike Joyce against Johnny Marr and Steven Morrissey was a simple one. He claimed that he was a partner in the Smiths between 1982 and 1987, and that as a result he was entitled to a 25% share of all profits arising out of their activities, (apart from songwriting and publishing income which he accepted belonged wholly to Marr and Morrissey).

His claim was based on section 24 of the Partnership Act 1890 which states:

The interests of partners in the partnership property and their rights and duties in relation to the partnership shall be determined, subject to any agreement express or implied between the partners by the following rules:

All the partners are entitled to share equally in the capital and profits of the business, and must contribute equally towards the losses whether of capital or otherwise sustained by the firm.

Joyce maintained that no express or implied agreement existed to contradict the above, and therefore all profits arising from recording and live performances should have been split four ways equally. However, the profits had in fact been split 40% (Morrissey), 40% (Marr), 10% (Rourke) and 10% (Joyce).

Initially, Andy Rourke was also a party to the proceedings however, apparently desperate for money, he withdrew before the case reached court, settling for the sum of £83,000 plus 10% of all future Smiths' royalties.

By the time the case reached court it was accepted by all parties that Joyce had been a partner in the Smiths and that the partnership had been dissolved on 31st of May 1987. However, Morrissey and Marr maintained that the unequal profit split was an implied term of the partnership.

Morrissey and Johnny Marr's defence

Steven Morrissey and Johnny Marr disputed Mike Joyce's case. They claimed that there was an agreement to split the profits 40% (Morrissey), 40% (Marr), 10% (Rourke) and 10% (Joyce), which had been inferred from conduct and had also been confirmed in a number of discussions. Their lawyer, Mr Rosen, put forward a range of evidence which, he claimed, proved that Joyce was aware of, and in agreement with, the unequal split, and confirmed their belief that they were not obliged to pay Joyce any more money.

- Morrissey and Marr asserted that they had acted as managers and organisers of the band and had therefore contributed far more to the band's success, and undergone far more stress, than Rourke and Joyce.

- Morrissey and Marr recounted that Marr had threatened to leave the band in 1983 because he was uncomfortable that Morrissey was insisting on the 40/40/10/10 split. However, Marr had actually been persuaded by Joyce to stay. Mr Rosen argued that this demonstrated Joyce's acceptance of the unequal split.

- Morrissey and Marr further stated that in 1984, whilst watching the Smiths on Top of the Pops in Mike Joyce's flat,

Marr had allegedly been asked by Joyce for an increase in his 10%. The request was rejected following a conversation with Morrissey. Mr Rosen maintained that the alleged request demonstrated that Joyce was fully aware of the unequal split.

- Morrissey observed that in 1986 Johnny Marr had advised him that Mike Joyce and Andy Rourke were angry that they were only receiving 10%; again they cited this as further evidence that Joyce and Rourke were aware of the unequal split.

- Morrissey alleged that in 1986 Joyce had offered to act as manager for the band in order to justify an increase in his share of the profits to 25%. He claimed that the conversation had taken place in a car journey between Manchester and London adding that the request had been rejected. Again, this was used as evidence that Joyce was aware of the unequal split.

- Morrissey claimed to have advised Mike Joyce that if he wasn't happy with his share of the profits he could leave the band. Joyce chose to stay.

- Morrissey and Marr stated that, having assumed that Joyce and Rourke had accepted the split, they had relied on the 40% split for their income.

- Morrissey and Marr referred to a set of accounts which was sent to Joyce in July 1986, which, they alleged, made the 40/40/10/10 split clear. They emphasised that Mike Joyce did not raise any objections or problems after receiving the accounts.

- Finally, Morrissey and Marr referred to a conversation which they suggested took place in 1987 in the kitchen of the Woolhall Studio. During the conversation their newly-appointed accountant, a Mr Savage, had asked Mr Rourke about his understanding of the profit split. Rourke replied that *"we get 10%."* Joyce made no comment or protest.

The court case

It was seven years before the case finally reached court.[12] Although Andy Rourke had settled his claim, he still gave evidence on behalf of Mike Joyce. During the court case, Morrissey made it clear that he saw himself and Johnny Marr as the key members of the Smiths. It was claimed that Morrissey referred to the drummer and bass player as *"mere session musicians as readily replaceable as the parts of a lawnmower."* He did not appear to dispute this concept. At one stage, he become quite angry and pointed to the title of Johnny Rogan's biography of the Smiths (*Morrissey & Marr: The Severed Alliance*):

> *There are only two names on the cover - Morrissey and Johnny Marr. Did you notice that? Two names only, not Michael Joyce or Andy Rourke.*

Mike Joyce claimed that he had always assumed that he was getting 25%, and that he had never examined, or understood, the royalty statements which had been sent to him. Even Morrissey's lawyer, Robert Englehart QC, admitted that:

> *Some 13 years on it is extremely difficult to pinpoint the moment when the 40%/40%/10%/10% profit split came into being.*

However he went on to say that:

> *Morrissey and Marr acted throughout on the basis that they would be getting 40 per cent each of the net profits from The Smiths' earnings.*

Mr Justice Weeks rejected the evidence relating to the conversations which were alleged to have taken place in 1986. He accepted the testimony from Mike Joyce, dismissing the suggestion that Johnny Marr had been in Joyce's flat in 1984 watching Top of the Pops. Morrissey admitted under cross-examination that, whilst he wanted the 40/40/40/10 split, the situation was still *"up in the air"* in 1984, as evidenced by discussions which subsequently took place with the band's solicitor and accountant.

Mr Justice Weeks also concluded that it was factually incorrect that Mr Rourke and Mr Joyce had *consistently* been receiving 10% of the profits from the recording and live activities of the band. He stated that there was no real pattern or consistency in the payments, with Joyce and Rourke actually receiving the same as Johnny Marr in some years.

The court was provided with documentary evidence from 1984, in the form of two letters from the band's solicitor, one to Scott Piering, the Smith's publicist, and one to Mrs Dwyer (Morrissey's mother). Morrissey admitted having discussed the letters with Johnny Marr. The first letter referred to the manner in which income from recordings and live performances was to be handled; it included the statement that all members of the band would *"in principle [...] be equally entitled to the net profits of the business."* In the second letter, the solicitor commented:

> *I was also concerned that there was no agreement between the individual members of the band. I took the view that as a matter of law the members of the Smiths were all equal partners although I was of course aware that this kind of arrangement was not acceptable to Morrissey or Johnny Marr.*

Finally, Morrissey admitted under cross-examination that a meeting had taken place in 1984 with the band's accountants, with all four band members present. During the meeting the split of profits was discussed, however no mention was made of the 40/40/10/10 proposal. Following this, the accountants had produced a set of draft accounts which split the income equally.

The hearing lasted seven days. In summing up, Mr Justice Weeks stated that he favoured the evidence of Joyce and Rourke, who he described as *"straightforward and honest, although without great intellectual ability."* His depiction of Morrissey was far less complimentary, and that depiction may have been more than partly to blame for the subsequent appeal:

> *Morrissey was more complicated and didn't find giving evidence easy or a happy experience. He was devious, truculent and unreliable when his own interests were at stake.*

As for Johnny Marr, the judge saw him as a more *"engaging"* and *"reasonable"* personality. He also described him as the most intelligent member of the band, a comment which would have undoubtedly infuriated Morrissey. However he tempered the compliments with the statement that Marr *"seemed to me to be willing to embroider his evidence to a point where he became less credible."*

The outcome was inevitable. The judge determined that there was no evidence of an agreement to split the profits 40/40/10/10, and there was no evidence that Joyce and Rourke had assumed that that was their entitlement. Following the decision, Mike Joyce commented:

> *I still have the highest regard for Morrissey but always knew 10 years ago when I started this action that I would win. This was never about money. It will not change my lifestyle but it will secure the future for my wife and children.*

The appeal

Johnny Marr decided not to appeal against the decision of the court however Morrissey chose to do so. The appeal was heard on 6 November 1998.[13] The argument put forward in the appeal by Morrissey's representative, Mr Rosen, was based on three factors:

- That Mr Justice Weeks had formed an unfairly negative view of Morrissey

- That this negative view led him to reject Morrissey's evidence relating to conversations about the split of profits

- That he failed to look in an overall manner at the question of whether an implied agreement existed to split the profits 40/40/10/10.

Mr Rosen suggested that the case should be decided by first examining the greater contribution made to the band by Morrissey and Marr, before considering evidence which supported the contention that an unequal split had been agreed.

Lord Justice Smith, leader of the Appeal Panel, firmly rejected the first part of this proposed approach. He emphasised that partnership law requires that profits always be distributed equally within a partnership, unless an agreement otherwise could be shown, regardless of the input of the partners. He quoted *Lindley and Banks on Partnership 17th edition* (Sweet & Maxwell: 1995) to support his standpoint:

> *Whether, therefore, partners have contributed money equally or unequally, whether or not they are on a par as regards skill, connection or character, whether they have or have not laboured equally for the benefit of the firm, their shares will be considered equal, unless some agreement to the contrary can be shown to have been entered into.*

Mr Rosen had supported the second part of his argument with two pieces of evidence which he felt strongly supported the claim:

- The Accounts sent to Mike Joyce in 1986, which provided a clear indication of a 40/40/10/10 split.

- The conversation that allegedly took place at Woolhall Studios in 1987, in front of Mike Joyce, during which Andy Rourke allegedly stated *"we get 10%"*.

However, in examining this evidence Lord Justice Smith concurred with the judgment of Mr Justice Weeks that the evidence did not support a conclusion that any implied agreement existed regarding an unequal split of profits:

> *...it was and is simply unsustainable that the partners were conducting their activities from the commencement of the partnership, and in any of the years 1983, 1984, 1985 or 1986 on a basis that the split should be 40%/40%/10%/10%. The maximum that could be said is that Mr Morrissey wanted to change the equal sharing to a 40%/40%/10%/10% split, but Mr Joyce and Mr Rourke were not happy to agree that change.*

He went on to stress that any change from the original manner in which the partnership had been operating (with profits split equally) would have to have been implemented in a transparent manner with the agreement of all partners. He highlighted the legal obligations which the partnership structure imposed:

> *it is not open to one partner by issuing an ultimatum that he is only continuing on the basis of a change in the distribution to achieve that change, if the other partners are equally making it clear that they do not accept that ultimatum.*

He dismissed Mr Rosen's suggestion that Mike Joyce's lack of response on receiving the 1986 accounts showing a 10% split consisted of agreement to an unequal split:

It is quite impossible to construe the sending of accounts by the partners' accountant as an offer that Mr Morrissey and Mr Marr were only prepared to continue on a 40%/40%/10%/10% basis, and quite impossible to construe Mr Joyce's silence as an acceptance of that offer.

He then considered the claim that the conversation at Woolhall studios confirmed Rourke and Joyce's acceptance of the unequal split. In the original hearing, Mr Justice Weeks had concluded that the conversation had not taken place, or, if it had, Mike Joyce had not heard it. However Lord Justice Smith went further, stating that it would have had no value even if it had taken place:

...it was not a conversation which was asserted as producing a variation, nor could it have been. It again came nowhere near to being an offer being made on behalf of Mr Morrissey and Mr Marr that they would only continue if Mr Joyce and Mr Rourke accepted their terms, and Mr Joyce's silence could in no way be construed as an acceptance. The conversation could be some confirmation that some agreement had already been reached. But for the reasons already given no previous agreement had been established.

Finally, Lord Justice Smith turned to Morrissey's state of mind observing that Morrissey might feel aggrieved that he and Johnny Marr had made a greater contribution to the band, had taken risks and responsibilities which the other members did not take, but had ended up with the same share of the profits. Without hearing the words spoken it is hard to detect whether there was any sympathy in his statement! Nevertheless, the outcome was the same; he dismissed the appeal and the two other members of the Appeal Panel concurred with his conclusion.

One other matter remained. In the initial case, Mr Justice Weeks had made an uncomplimentary observation about Morrissey:

Mr Morrissey is a more complicated character. He did not find giving evidence an easy or happy experience. To me at least he appeared devious, truculent and unreliable where his own interests were at stake.

Lord Justice Smith commented briefly on this, partly as a response to Mr Rosen's contention that the judge's decision had been influenced by an unfairly negative opinion of Morrissey:

All [...] the judge intended to convey in his use of the word devious was that Mr Morrissey had not faced up to Mr Joyce and Mr Rourke with an ultimatum, and sought to bring about inequality by indirect means.

A second member of the panel, Lord Justice Thorpe, addressed this in much more depth and detail, and his comments are worth reproducing in full:

A distinction is to be drawn between an assessment of credibility, an assessment of demeanour and an assessment of personality. In my opinion the judge in the passages under review was stating his assessment of Mr Morrissey's credibility. In arriving at a low assessment he relied in part upon an assessment of his demeanour. [...] I read the three adjectives selected by the judge as restricted to his demeanour whilst testifying. To label a witness unreliable is one of the more merciful ways to rejecting his testimony. [...] The label of truculence Mr Rosen accepted was not unwarranted given a number of uncooperative exchanges between Mr Morrissey and his cross examiner. So if the judge went further than he needed to go or than he was entitled to go it was in saying that Mr Morrissey had given him the impression of being devious. This has been understood by the appellant to be a general and moralistic judgment not only of his conduct of the litigation but also of his conduct throughout the duration of the partnership. I have already sought to explain my firm opinion that that was not the judge's meaning. I am quite clear that the judge was expressing no more than an impression of the value of Mr Morrissey's oral evidence.

Lord Justice Thorpe made further observations about the manner in which Morrissey gave evidence and responded under questioning, suggesting that he *"forfeited the judge's sympathy"* by engaging in a *"war of words"* with the cross-examiner, rather than answering questions in a manner that was *"clear, relevant and helpful to the judge."* He suggested that such an attitude was not unusual in witnesses but rarely positive. Given Morrissey's character and fondness for controversial public pronouncements, one can certainly imagine him taking part in such exchanges.

The third member of the panel, Lord Justice Peter Gibson, recognised that the appeal may have been motivated by the judge's assessment of Morrissey. However, he concurred with the other members of the panel that Mr Justice Weeks did not mean that Morrissey was dishonest.

So after a trial and appeal, Mike Joyce won his case, and Morrissey and Marr were required to pay future and past royalties to him.

Analysis

Inevitably there are differing perspectives about the royalty dispute which the Smiths were embroiled in. Some observers might feel that Morrissey and Marr got what they deserved, having tried to short-change their ex-partners. Others might feel that it was unfair for a drummer and bass player, who contributed far less creatively and managerially to the band, to receive the same rewards as Morrissey and Marr, the instigators of, and driving forces within, the band. It should be emphasised that, as joint song-writers, Morrissey and Marr will have received all the publishing income, and this is likely to have amounted to substantially more than the income from recording and live activities. Income from recording and live activities also tends to decline after the band has split up (see the *Spandau Ballet* case in Chapter 7 for a clear illustration of this phenomenon), whereas Morrissey and Marr would have continued to benefit from the publishing income stream after the break up. It should also be highlighted that the court was not required to make judgments about what was fair. It was simply asked to judge the facts of the case in light of the relevant law, which, in the circumstances, was the Partnership Act of 1890.

It was not surprising that Morrissey and Marr lost. Their case could only have been successful if they had demonstrated that there was an implied agreement that there should be an unequal split of income. There was no real robust evidence to prove that.

Epilogue

Sorrow will come in the end was Morrissey's musical response to the court case, though it was not released on the UK version of *Maladjusted*, and it is now difficult find a recorded version. He also made some other public comments about the case. For example, when asked after the court case if Rourke and Joyce had had a bad deal he replied:

> *They were lucky. If they'd had another singer they'd never have got further than Salford shopping centre.*[14]

Dispute continued over payment of back-royalties to Mike Joyce. In November 2005, in an interview with Marc Riley on BBC Radio 6, Joyce explained that he was selling some rare Smiths' material on eBay because he needed the money. He also referred to "*being skint and selling everything*" in the 90s.

This led to a public statement from Morrissey, published on the *True to You* fanzine site in 2005. In the statement he claimed that he and Johnny Marr had each paid £215,000 to Joyce in 1997, and that Marr had made a final payment of back royalties of £260,000 plus costs in 2001. He stated that he had not been served with court proceedings because he had been in the US, but that Joyce had subsequently obtained a Default Judgment and served him with a claim for £688,000. He then went on to state that since 2001 Joyce had undertaken Third Party orders (amounting to a *further* £700,000) against his personal bank account in England, against Smiths' royalties from Warner Music and against his personal PRS & PPL royalties. He also alleged that Joyce had attempted to take UK concert fees owed to him and had attempted to seize UK houses belonging to his sister and mother (actions which were later dropped). He claimed that defending these (and other) claims had cost him £600,000 in legal fees.

Morrissey maintained that Joyce had deprived others (including Andy Rourke) from their entitlements by taking the full value of Smiths' royalties from Warner Music, having allegedly failed to declare to courts that others were also beneficiaries. His calculation was that Joyce had cost him "*1 million, 515 thousand pounds*" and continued to cost him £100 per day in interest. He finished his statement with the observation:

> *Joyce is not poor, unless, living as he does in the Cheshire green-belt, he lives beyond his means. Somehow, he appears to believe that he should have equal financial status to both myself and to Johnny Marr, even though Joyce has done dramatically less than Johnny and I to attain the positions we now have. Joyce is not poor because of one reason - me. His career now is the fictitious position of an unpaid ex-member of the Smiths.*[15]

At a concert in 2008, Morrissey advised his fans not to buy the Smiths' back catalogue as all the money would go to that "*wretched drummer.*" Unsurprisingly, Joyce's view was different. In an interview, he stated that Morrissey had owed him money, and was refusing to pay it on the grounds that he lived in the US and the UK judgment did not apply there. Strangely, when asked during an interview in 2007 about a Smith's reunion performance, Joyce suggested that it might be possible one day. Morrissey clearly had other ideas, allegedly remarking in 2006:

> *I would rather eat my own testicles than reform the Smiths; and that's saying something for a vegetarian.*[16]

In 2013, Morrissey was rather more successful in a legal dispute, when he won £10,000 from Channel 4 after they played a Smiths' track without permission on a trailer for a Gordon Ramsey cookery show. Morrissey was particularly put out by the use of the track, because of Ramsey's attitude towards vegetarianism. Morrissey donated the payment to *"People for the Ethical Treatment of Animals (PETA)"*, to fund a fight against the production of foie gras.[17]

CONTRACTS AND FIDUCIARY DUTY

TAKE THAT

Take That were created in 1990 by an entrepreneur named Nigel Martin-Smith. Martin-Smith's first venture into business was when he opened a model and acting agency in 1981. From 1984 onwards, he became more involved in popular music. He believed that there was an opportunity for a clean-living boy band, made up of *"English boys with strong and likeable personalities."* Through auditions and contacts he selected the five boys who would become *Take That*: Mark Owen; Howard Donald; Jason Orange; Gary Barlow; and Robbie Williams. He then set to work with the boys to train them and develop their image. He wanted them to appear hard-working, intelligent and well-behaved, and without girlfriends.

On October 29th 1990 a formal management agreement was signed between Martin-Smith and all five members of the group. Martin-Smith ensured that the five members were all given independent legal advice. The agreement appointed him *"to act as our sole and exclusive manager in connection with all our activities in all branches of entertainment."* Under the terms of the management agreement, he was entitled to 25% commission on the gross receipts of all members of the group.

The agreement lasted for an initial period of three years. It was then extended, in line with an option available to Martin-Smith, for a further two years, to terminate on October 29th 1995. Negotiations were taking place to extend the contract during 1995. It was claimed by Martin-Smith that a verbal agreement had been made in May 1995 that it would be extended indefinitely, subject to six months' notice on either side, in return for a reduction in his commission from 25% to 20%.

The group formally split up on February 13th 1996. The announcement went down badly with their millions of fans, some of whom threatened suicide; special telephone help-lines were set up to help ease their distress. However four members of the group reformed ten years later in 2006, and Robbie Williams re-joined them in 2010. They undertook further sell-out tours and released successful recordings.

As at November 2012, the group has had 11 number one singles, and 5 number one studio albums in the UK, as well as 54 number one singles and 3 number one albums internationally. The album they released after all five were back together, *Progress*, became the fastest selling album of the century on its first day of sales, November 15th 2010. A further album is apparently in preparation.

The legal dispute in this case study occurred after Robbie Williams fell out with the other group members and left the group in July 1995. Following his departure Martin-Smith was not paid commission on his earnings. As a result, he took legal action against Williams demanding damages for breach of the Agreement, and commission on earnings between August 1995 and February 1996, the date at which six months' notice would have expired had Williams served notice to leave in line with the alleged verbal agreement. The case was heard in the High Court, Chancery Division, before Mr Justice Ferris, in July 1997. A full transcript of the judgment, which provides some useful and detailed insights into the discussions and contract between Martin-Smith and the group, and from which the extracts below have been drawn, can be seen at *Martin-Smith v Williams [1998] EMLR 334*.

Robbie Williams' first defence

Mr Silverleaf, the representative for Robbie Williams, put forward two alternative defences in response to Martin-Smith's claim.

In the first of these he claimed that the Agreement was terminated on July 13th or August 11th 1995 by Williams' acceptance of a *repudiatory* breach of the agreement by Martin-Smith.

Repudiatory breach

A repudiatory or fundamental breach of a contract is defined as:

a breach so fundamental that it permits the distressed party to terminate performance of the contract, in addition to entitling that party to sue for damages.[18]

Clause 3 of the Management Agreement which Nigel Martin-Smith had signed with each of the members of *Take That* stated that he would "*use all reasonable endeavours*" to develop the careers of each of the members of the group in the entertainment industry. Mr Silverleaf, Robbie Williams' representative, claimed that this imposed a *fiduciary* duty upon Martin-Smith to act in Robbie Williams' best interests at all times in promoting his career within the entertainment field. He maintained that the advice Martin-Smith gave to the other members of the group regarding their dealings with Williams put him in conflict with Williams' interests. He continued by arguing that this conflict was a repudiatory breach of the Management Agreement, and Williams was therefore entitled to walk away from it in July 1995, without giving any notice, and without any obligation to pay commission to Martin-Smith on his earnings after that date.

Mr Justice Ferris therefore had to examine in detail the discussions and events which took place in July 1995, in the lead up to Robbie Williams' departure.

After a relatively slow start, sales of the group's recordings took off from June 1992 and they became hugely successful from then through to 1994. The first indication that there were problems ahead with Robbie Williams came in the middle of 1994. The other group members were becoming increasingly worried about his behaviour which included drug abuse which apparently almost led him to a drug overdose the night before the group were due to play at the MTV Europe Music awards ceremony. At first Martin-Smith allowed them to sort things out amongst themselves but things got worse in early 1995. As a result, Gary Barlow suggested to Martin-Smith that a meeting should be held "*to sort Robbie out.*" In an attempt to avoid making Williams feel victimised, Martin-Smith arranged a group meeting on January 23rd 1995. This led to a written set of seven "*band rules*". This seemed to bring about a positive change in the atmosphere and relationships; plans were put in place for rehearsals throughout July and performances in Manchester and London in August. A six week international tour was also planned for September and October.

However the situation had deteriorated again by the end of June, and the other four members of the group met with Martin-Smith on June 28th to complain again about Williams' attitude and behaviour. Things had got so bad that rehearsals had been abandoned early, and some members of the group were demanding that Williams be thrown out. The series of meetings and discussions which took place over the following two weeks were key to Mr Justice Ferris's judgment of the claim for repudiatory breach.

June 29th, 1995 - Martin-Smith discussed the situation with his solicitor, Mr Kennedy, who advised him that he had to act carefully and fairly as he managed all members of the group, and he should not under any circumstances dismiss Williams from the group.

June 30th, 1995 - A meeting for the entire group was arranged at Gary Barlow's house however Robbie Williams did not arrive at the agreed time so the other group members discussed the situation with Martin-Smith on his own. Jason Orange and Gary Barlow were keen to throw Williams out. When Williams arrived the discussion became heated, and it was suggested that he should leave the group. Martin-Smith suggested that they should all go home and think about it, and try to get back to rehearsing. He was hopeful that the situation would settle down.

July 11th, 1995 - Martin-Smith returned from holiday, and discovered that matters had not improved. He was advised that Robbie Williams had informed the group at a meeting on July 8th that he would be leaving the group in January 1996.

July 12th, 1995 - Following a function in Manchester, (which the whole group attended), Martin-Smith met with Gary Barlow and Jason Orange, at Barlow's house. Barlow and Orange were insistent that Williams should be asked to leave the group, whereas Martin-Smith gave his strong opinion that they should try to work with him. Finally, Martin-Smith suggested that they should offer Williams two alternatives: to commit himself wholeheartedly to the tour, or, if he was determined to leave, to do so immediately so that he could get on with his other plans, and the group could re-establish themselves without him. In his evidence, Martin-Smith maintained that he had emphasised to Orange and Barlow that they could not sack Williams, they could only offer him the different options.

July 13th, 1995 - The five group members met (without Martin-Smith). They explained the content of the discussion with Martin-Smith, and the options which they had agreed to offer him. He responded by saying *"Ok then, I'm not going to carry on rehearsing - I'm off."* He then left the rehearsals and the group continued without him.

43

July 13th, 1995 - Martin-Smith wrote to his solicitor, Mr Kennedy, to advise him that Robbie Williams had left the group. He relayed the conversation which he had had with Jason Orange and Gary Barlow as follows:

> *It was decided that the band would have another meeting with Robbie to ask him if he had reconsidered his decision to leave in January. I advised that if he had they should encourage him to get involved again and we should then draw up some form of agreement for the next twelve months but that if he was adamant that he was going I suggested that they encourage him to go straight away.*

August 11th, 1995 - Robbie Williams' solicitors wrote to Martin-Smith's solicitor, alleging that Martin-Smith had breached his fiduciary duty to Williams and had induced the other group members to breach the terms of their partnership with Robbie Williams. The letter referred to meeting which took place without Williams on July 12th, claiming that *"the result of that meeting was the decision to sack our client."* The letter stated that Robbie Williams was entitled to terminate the Management Agreement with immediate effect, as a result of the repudiatory breach of the Agreement by Martin-Smith.

A year later, on August 6th, 1996, Martin-Smith issued the writ against Robbie Williams.

Judgment on the first defence

Although the letter of August 11th stated that a decision had been made at the meeting of July 12th to *"sack"* Robbie Williams, no evidence or argument was presented in the court to support the claim. In any event Mr Justice Ferris made it clear that he rejected any suggestion that Martin-Smith had advised Barlow and Orange to sack Williams. Furthermore he accepted Martin-Smith's account that he had advised Gary Barlow and Jason Orange that they should offer Robbie Williams TWO options: to leave the group immediately or to stay with the group long-term. His advice had emphasised that the second of these options would require a high level of commitment to the group, and an agreement to be signed for at least the next twelve months.

Robbie Williams' representative in court, Mr Silverleaf, highlighted a discrepancy between the witness statement of Martin-Smith in which he said that he had advised the other members that they *"should offer him the option of going straight away, so that he need not work out his notice if he did not want to"* and the letter of July 13th in which he stated that *"if he was adamant that he was going I suggested that they encourage him to go straight away."* Mr Silverleaf suggested that the difference between *"offer him the option"*, compared to *"encourage"* demonstrated that Martin-Smith had deliberately changed the emphasis, using more neutral terms in his witness statement than had been used in the original letter. However, Mr Justice Ferris did not see these differences in the language used as important:

> *I do not think that this was a fair criticism of Martin-Smith. It is impossible now to be sure of the precise language used by Martin-Smith in advising Gary Barlow and Jason Orange on July 12. The letter to Kennedy does not purport to be a verbatim account. In any event I am not satisfied that, in the context, there is a distinction of significance between "offer him the option of going straight away" and "encourage him to go straight away". This is because of the existence of the alternative option (expressed in the witness statement as "encourage him to get involved again permanently and commit himself to the group" and in the letter simply as "encourage him to get involved again"). Even if the letter is to be preferred to the oral evidence, so that the proposal was put in terms of "encourage" him to go rather than "offer him the option" to go, then the language of the encouragement to leave was no more emphatic than that of the encouragement to get involved again.*

The Judge did agree that, *had* Martin-Smith encouraged the others to dismiss Williams then it *would* have been a breach of his obligations to develop William's career as contained in Clause 3 of the Management Contract. However he did not believe that this had happened.

Mr Justice Ferris then examined the question of *"fiduciary duty."* He observed that both parties accepted that the relationship between Martin-Smith and Robbie Williams *was* fiduciary, because of the degree of control which Martin-Smith had over Williams' business affairs, and because of the need for continued trust and confidence between them. It was further agreed that the same relationship existed between Martin-Smith and the other four group members. This led to a discussion of how a 'fiduciary" could ensure that they did not breach their fiduciary duty when acting for more than one client. The court referred to the case of *Bristol & West Building Society v Mothew [1996],* which established three rules relating to fiduciary duties:

The *"double employment"* rule which requires that the fiduciary does not act for two principals with potentially conflicting interests, because then his duty to one principal may conflict with his duty to the other.

The *"duty of good faith"* rule which requires that a fiduciary acting for two clients with potentially conflicting interests must always act in good faith in the interests of each client, and must never favour one client's interest at the expense of the other. As Lord Justice Millett put it:

> *But it goes further than this. He must not allow the performance of his obligations to one principal to be influenced by his relationship with the other. He must serve each as faithfully and loyally as if he were his only principal.*[19]

The *"no conflict"* rule which requires that the fiduciary avoided reaching a position of *actual* conflict of duty, which would mean that he cannot fulfil his obligations to one principal without failing in his obligations to the other.

Mr Justice Ferris did not accept that Martin-Smith was in breach of the *double employment* rule. He believed that he was appointed manager of **each** of the five members of the group individually, as well as manager of the group as a whole, and fulfilled his obligations to all of them in his advice to the other group members about how they should deal with Robbie Williams' desire to leave the group, without betraying his obligation to Williams himself.

Mr Justice Ferris also did not accept that Martin-Smith had breached the *duty of good faith* rule:

> *I cannot see how the advice which I have found Martin-Smith to have given to Gary Barlow and Jason Orange can be said to have affected the performance of his duties to Robbie Williams. If the group was to continue as before it was as important to Robbie Williams as it was to the other members of the group that the forthcoming tours should be successful. Apart from the damage to the reputation of the group, there would be serious adverse financial consequences to all the members of the group if for any reason the group failed to fulfil its commitments. Secondly Martin-Smith clearly believed that the avoidance of these consequences required that matters were resolved immediately, either on the basis of a long-term commitment of the group to each other or on the basis of an immediate break. I am sure that if the occasion had arisen Martin-Smith would have given the same advice to all the members of the group, both collectively and individually.*

Finally, Mr Justice Ferris believed that Martin-Smith was not in breach of the *actual conflict* rule. He saw no conflict between the advice which Martin-Smith gave to Gary Barlow and Jason Orange and the interests of Robbie Williams. He clearly believed that things could have proved more difficult for Martin-Smith had the other group members asked him a different question:

It might well have been different if Martin-Smith had been asked to advise them whether, and if so how, they could dismiss Robbie Williams from the group. But Martin-Smith knew very well, from the advice of Kennedy if not also from his own instinct, that he could not do this. In my judgment he was not asked to do it and did not do it.

One question raised by Williams' representative related to the manner in which Martin-Smith's comments were delivered to Williams by the other group members. However, Mr Justice Ferris did not see this as something which could be used as evidence of breach of the agreement by Martin-Smith:

It may be that they did not accurately convey to Robbie Williams the advice of Martin-Smith, but that is not something which can be blamed on Martin-Smith.

The Judge therefore concluded that it would be *"illogical"* to suggest that the advice given by Martin-Smith to Barlow and Orange was a breach of his duty to Williams.

Robbie Williams' second defence

The second defence put forward by Mr Silverleaf on Robbie Williams' behalf was that the Agreement between Martin-Smith & *Take That* was not extended in May 1995 and thus ended on October 29th 1995.

Discussions about extending the Management Agreement had started in early 1995. Martin-Smith was concerned that it was coming to an end in October 1995, as he had invested efforts and finance in setting up an organisation to look after the group's affairs. The question of Martin-Smith's rate of commission also formed part of these discussions.

Martin-Smith and all the members of the group met in Manchester on May 15th 1995, in a meeting attended by independent solicitors. There were two key outcomes to the meeting:

- It was agreed that Martin-Smith would accept 20 per cent in place of 25 per cent from January 1st 1994.

- It was proposed by Martin-Smith, and agreed by all parties, that the Management Agreement should continue indefinitely but be subject to termination by any party on giving six months' notice.

Mr Silverleaf accepted that the extension was agreed in principle at the Manchester meeting, however he maintained that the agreement had been "subject to contract", and argued that a binding contractual agreement had never been reached.

Judgment on the second defence

Mr Justice Ferris summarised the key points of the evidence relating to the agreement extension as follows:

- Nothing was said at the meeting about the agreement being subject to contract.

- Nothing express was said about the agreement being an immediate binding agreement.

- Subsequently there were interchanges between Mr Babbington (on behalf of the group members) and Mr Bray (on behalf of Martin-Smith) about the contract. A letter from Bray was marked *"subject to contract."* The letters

Babbington had sent suggested that a binding agreement *had* been formed.

- On September 21st 1995 the other four members of the group and Martin-Smith entered into a formal agreement.

Mr Justice Ferris was plain that he put more weight on the first of these points rather than the second, and in confirming so was rather scathing about Robbie Williams' representative, observing:

> *Mr Silverleaf also established, somewhat laboriously, that nothing express was said about the agreement being an immediate binding agreement. Mr Silverleaf's point seems to me to be of no significance. Parties who reach agreement intended to be immediately binding rarely, if ever, go on to say expressly that this is their intention.*

He was also candid about the significance of the contradictory views of the solicitors, as expressed in their correspondence:

> *Mr Babbington's state of mind is, like that of Mr Bray, of limited relevance.*

The Judge also saw the fact that the remaining four members of the group had signed a written agreement on September 21st to be of no relevance when considering whether or not the oral agreement of May 15th was binding.

As a result of all the above factors, he concluded that the verbal agreement was binding on Robbie Williams and concluded with a statement which would later be cited as precedent in future cases relating to oral agreements:

> *The extension of the Management Agreement was something which was capable of being the subject of an oral agreement. In my view if, in relation to such a matter, parties reach accord by means of offer*

and acceptance then they should be treated as contractually bound to each other unless it is shown that either or both of the offer or the acceptance which lead to such accord are subject to a condition which prevents them being legally bound. Typically such a condition will be that the accord is "subject to contract", in which case neither party will be bound unless and until a written contract between them is prepared and signed.

Commission and damages

As a result of the Judge's decision, the Management Agreement was considered to have continued until 10th February 1996, six months after Martin-Smith's solicitors had received the letter from Williams. The Judge did make a passing comment that Martin-Smith might have argued that Williams' letter of August 11th 1996 was not valid as six months' notice as it was not given on behalf of the whole group. Had that argument been successful, then presumably Martin-Smith would have been able to suggest that the Agreement was still in place, and claim further commission and damages. However, having somewhat mischievously, and some might say unnecessarily, raised it, the Judge then dismissed it on the grounds that Martin-Smith had accepted the letter as six months' notice.

As a result of the judgment, Martin-Smith would be entitled to 20% commission on the earnings of Robbie Williams until 10th February 1996. However, he might also be entitled to damages in respect of his breach of the Management Agreement. This damages would compensate him for earnings which he might have gained had the Agreement been honoured by Williams.

In theory, the first of these would be relatively easy to calculate. However, there were a couple of complications, which Mr Justice Ferris would need to consider and make judgment upon.

BMG complication

The first of these related to BMG Records Limited. *Take That* had entered a recording agreement with BMG, however after leaving the group, Robbie Williams had attempted to extract himself from this agreement. Following legal proceedings and negotiations a settlement was reached whereby, in return for being released from the agreement, Williams waived commission due to him to a value of £450,000. This figure was made up of two sums. The first of these amounted to £250,000 relating to commission due to Williams on the release of *"the Hits"* album. This matched an estimate of BMG's legal costs which Williams was due to pay as a result of the proceedings which had taken place in order to extract himself from the agreement with them. The second amount was £200,000 relating to commission on any royalties due on other *Take That* recordings. This appeared to be compensation to BMG for him terminating the agreement early. After ending the agreement with BMG, Williams entered a new agreement with Chrysalis Records Limited. Williams' representative argued that Martin-Smith was not entitled to commission on the sum of £450,000 because *"it has not been and will not be received by or credited to Robbie Williams or any entity controlled by him."*

Importantly, clause 5 of the Management Agreement between Martin-Smith and the members of *Take That* had provided a thorough and all-encompassing definition of *"commissionable monies"* as:

> *... all gross monies or other considerations (exclusive of VAT or any similar taxes) whether received by or credited to us or received by or credited to a person, company, firm or other entity acting on our behalf or controlled directly or indirectly by us or otherwise received for or credited to our benefit during or after the Term and which arise out of any activities referred to in Clause 1 which are undertaken by us as a result of any contract or other arrangement*

entered into or substantially negotiated during the Term or in replacement or substitution for a contract or arrangement existing during the Term or which arise in respect of our activities in the entertainment industry prior to or during the Term.

As the original recording agreement between BMG and the members of the group was signed during the term of the Management Agreement, then any sums paid or credited by BMG to Robbie Williams under the recording agreement were *"commissionable monies."* The questions which Mr Justice Ferris believed he needed to consider were:

Has Robbie Williams has prevented the total sum of £450,000 from being 'commissionable monies?'

If so, has he done so without being in breach of any express or implied term of the Management Agreement?

Had the Judge had answered yes to both questions, then Williams would have succeeded in avoiding 20% commission on £450,000. The Judge dealt with the two amounts dealt separately.

With regard to the first amount, Williams' case was that the £250,000 was never credited to him as it had never been paid to him or put in account he could access. A further argument put forward by Williams' representative was that the amount equated to a recoupable deduction which BMG were entitled to take under the terms of their contract with Williams, and was therefore not *"commissionable money."*

Mr Justice Ferris dismissed these arguments, He did not accept the submission that *"clause 5(a) of the Management Agreement includes within commissionable monies only monies which had actually become payable by BMG to Robbie Williams."*

He felt that the position regarding the £200,000 was less straightforward as it was not specifically stated what it related to. However he determined that the **substance** was more important than the **form** of the agreement - it may not have said it was payment of royalties, but in reality that was what it was.

Overall the Judge concluded that Williams had not prevented the £450,000 becoming commissionable. Logically, there was no need to address the second question however, for the sake of completeness, and for clarity in the case of appeal, he did so. His conclusion was that, by waiving the amount of money due from BMG as part of his settlement, Williams had broken clause 5 (c) of the Management Agreement which stated:

We confirm that we have not assigned or charged and will not, without your prior consent, assign or charge to any third party any advances, fees, royalties, monies or other considerations to which we may have been or become entitled or to which we may hereafter become entitled.

Greatest Hits complication

The second "*complication*" related to a book entitled *Take That--Our Greatest Hits* which was published by Virgin in 1996. The issue was whether Martin-Smith was entitled to commission on Robbie Williams' earnings from the book.

The book resulted from an agreement made between Virgin and a company named *Take That Performance Limited*. The formal agreement was signed after February 10th 1996 – the date now agreed as the termination date of the Management Agreement. The book itself was published around March 25th 1996. However, the representative for Martin-Smith claimed that the agreement was "*substantially negotiated*" before February 10th 1996 and also argued that the book portrayed Williams' "*activities in the entertainment industry prior to or during the term"* and income from the book should therefore be commissionable monies.

In examining the first of these arguments, there was correspondence showing that negotiations had taken place with Virgin in December 1995 and January 1996, and that an outline proposal had been produced. However, Virgin's acceptance of the proposal was linked to the negotiation of *"a clear and very tight first option"* on two other books, and needed agreement of Robbie Williams. A letter of February 5th 1996 from Martin-Smith's solicitor to Robbie Williams' solicitor asking for agreement did not receive a reply until later in the month, sometime after February 10th. New terms which had not previously been mentioned were introduced into the agreement. As a result, the Judge concluded that the contract for the sale of the book was not substantially negotiated before February 10th 1996, and accordingly Martin-Smith was not entitled to commission on Williams' share

The alternative argument was also rejected by the Judge. Commenting, possibly tongue in cheek, that he had *"not myself studied the book in any detail"* he went on to accept that the events within it related to the period when the Management Agreement was in place. However, he then stated

> *I do not consider that the royalties payable to Robbie Williams arise from these events or photographs. They arise from the information and other material contained in the book. Even treating the presentation of this information and material as an "activity in the entertainment industry" it cannot, in my view, be regarded as an activity carried out before the date of publication of the book.*

Having lost on the major elements of the case, Williams had won on the final, minor item. However, the Judge made an order for an inquiry as to damages to be paid to Martin-Smith for the defendant's breach of contract, as well as an account of the commissionable monies due to Martin-Smith.

A number of key points are illustrated by the *Take That* case.

Verbal agreements are binding

Verbal contracts are binding just like written contracts. The difficulty is proving what exactly was agreed. It is possible to make a verbal agreement *"subject to contract"*, but it needs to be clear that this is what the parties intend.

Fiduciary duty

The Manager of a group has a difficult job. He or she has a fiduciary duty to all the individual members of the group and has to tread carefully when giving advice to them to demonstrate objectivity and fairness. Mr Martin-Smith undertook that duty in a professional and measured manner, and that ensured that he could not be judged to have betrayed that fiduciary duty when Robbie Williams decided to leave the group. It would have been quite easy to have fallen into the trap of favouring one group member over another.

Documentation and attention to detail

Documenting correspondence and meetings can be extremely important. Ensuring that documentation is correct is also essential. Clauses within contracts need to be carefully worded. Had the clause regarding commission not been comprehensive then Robbie Williams might have avoided paying commission which, in fairness, he was due to pay. Dates can also be critical – if Robbie Williams' solicitor had agreed to the Virgin contract before Feb 10th then Williams might have ended up paying commission on the book.

Repudiatory breach

A repudiatory breach is a breach of a *"condition"* within a contract. A *"condition"* is something which is essential to the contract. It may not always be obvious. However, if something is, from your point of view, critical to the contract then you can specify that it is a condition of the contract. For example, if you order some merchandise for a show then it is clearly essential that is delivered *prior* to the show, so you should be explicit that the delivery date is a condition of the contract. If your supplier delivers late then you would be entitled to with-hold payment in full, on the grounds that it was a *"repudiatory"* breach of the contract.

Fair and reasonable contracts

Some might wonder why the contract which Martin-Smith had was so short. Initially it was just two years, but then he took out an option for a further three years. That still left him quite exposed, given that he would have had to invest time and money in developing the band and they could simply have left after five years. In reality, however, it was sensible, as lengthy contracts have been found in the past to be unenforceable, especially when signed with inexperienced and young artists. His strategy of accepting a reduction in commission in return for a rolling contract also appeared to be a fair approach.

Was it worth it?

A final question which might be asked is whether Robbie Williams should have simply paid up, rather than attempted to defend his position. He certainly would have saved legal costs, and Martin-Smith might have settled for a lower damages figure. It did seem surprising given the Judge's comments and decisions that he decided to appeal. But he did.

The appeal

Robbie Williams decided to appeal against the Judge's decisions on three grounds:

(1) repudiatory breach

(2) the monies retained by BMG

(3) the order for an inquiry as to damages for breach of the management agreement.

The Appeal was held before Lord Justices Beldam, Roch and Mummery, in March 1999.[20]

Repudiatory breach

The representative for Williams maintained that Martin-Smith had taken sides with the other members of the group when the difficulties arose in the middle of 1995. He argued that Martin-Smith had given them advice which was not in Williams' best interest and by doing so, had lost William's trust and confidence. He contended that, as a result, Martin-Smith had repudiated the Management Agreement, and Williams was entitled to walk away without giving notice.

The three Appeal Judges did not accept this argument. Lord Justice Mummery observed that Martin-Smith had been appointed by the group to act on their behalf, and to consider the interests of the group before the interests of individuals. He felt that Martin-Smith had done this in an appropriate and equitable manner:

> *There was no conflict between that advice and the interests of the defendant. The advice did not affect the performance of the plaintiff's duties to the defendant. The advice was that the*

defendant should be given the option of staying or of going straight away. It was a reasonable option. The plaintiff did not abandon the defendant, who, in his own interests, chose to leave the group immediately.

The first ground for appeal was therefore dismissed.

The money retained by BMG

Robbie William's representative maintained that Williams was entitled to make an agreement with BMG which resulted in reduced royalties, as otherwise the Management Agreement would have imposed a restraint of trade upon him, by preventing him from dealing with his royalties as he wished. He also repeated the argument that the waived royalties were not commissionable monies. However, the Appeal Judges did not accept these arguments either. Lord Justice Mummery observed:

The defendant received the benefit of being credited with sums which, but for the waiver by him in favour of BMG, would have been received by him from BMG. [...] They are "commissionable monies" within clause 5(a).

Inquiry as to damages

The Judge in the initial case ordered an inquiry as to damages for the defendant's breach of contract, as well as an account of commission due for the period up to 10 February 1996. the commissionable monies. The defendant objected, arguing that no damages had been claimed or suffered by Martin-Smith, and that he should not be entitled to both commission under the Management Agreement, and damages for breach of contract.

The Appeal Judges maintained that there was a claim for damages, and that Martin-Smith *had* suffered potential loss as a result of missing the opportunity to earn commission from new contracts which might have been agreed during the six month period when Williams was not accepting that he was managed by him.

Lord Justice Mummery did not see any difficulty with this sitting alongside a claim for commission, observing:

> *There is no inconsistency in having an account in order to calculate the commission in respect of contracts concluded and an inquiry as to damages for loss of the opportunity to earn commission on contracts not concluded.*

Overall, the Appeal process only resulted in additional legal costs for Robbie Williams as he failed on all of the three grounds which were put forward.

Epilogue

The Evening Standard reported that Robbie Williams had to pay £90,000 commission due on *Take That* earnings, plus an estimated £500,000 commission on his own earnings to February 1996, plus an estimated £500,000 in court costs. Having had differing levels of success in their solo careers, *Take That* reformed in 2006 and went on to record several more successful albums.

Nigel Martin-Smith undertook a number of varied and successful projects including:

- Managing the comeback of Lulu

- Setting up the NMSM Talent Group in Manchester incorporating a talent agency (Urban Talent); a management company for actors (Lime Actors); and two fashion and photographic model agencies (Nemesis Models and Smith's)

- Owning three gay bars in Manchester's gay village on Canal Street

- Co-owning a Funeral Directors

In 2005, he was engaged when *Take That* reunited as a four-piece group. He co-produced a documentary about the group, managed the release of a compilation album, *The Ultimate Collection*, and launched the UK tour. However he was sacked before the tour began. Mark Owen commented that there was no role for him, but many assumed that the reason for his sacking lay in the continuing dispute with Robbie Williams.

Williams' biography, published in 2004, referred to Martin-Smith as *"the spawn of Satan"* and blamed him for destroying his self-confidence and telling people he was gay. Martin-Smith responded by suggesting that the difficulties Williams had suffered with drugs and alcohol were rooted in his inability to deal with his sexuality.

The 2006 solo album, *Rudebox*, contained a track called The 90s, whose threatening lyrics originally stated:

> *Either you're a thief or you're shit, which one will you admit to?*
> *Such an evil man, I used to fantasise about taking a Stanley knife*
> *and playing around with your eyes.*

Martin-Smith undertook legal action against Williams and EMI before the album was released, and the lyrics were rewritten. Eventually the dispute ended up in court, however, and Robbie Williams was required to pay damages to Martin-Smith, estimated by newspapers at £300,000, and to formally apologise to him, through an official statement read out by his lawyer:

> *Robbie Williams wishes to make it clear to his fans, and the public*
> *at large, that he did not intend these lyrics to be taken at face value*

or as a serious statement by him of the views which he holds of Nigel Martin Smith. Specifically, Robbie Williams did not intend to allege that Nigel Martin Smith has ever stolen any funds from Take That or anyone.[21]

Martin-Smith claimed that he had tried to settle the matter with Williams out of court, but Williams refused to meet him:

I told Robbie I didn't want damages and that I would happily waive them if he would meet me face to face to chat about what has happened and put all this negativity behind us. I said we should just be friends again. But he refused to meet me. I then said I would accept him giving me a written undertaking to read a letter I would have written setting out my thoughts on everything that had happened. But he refused once again. So now he has to pay me damages. It's a real shame it has come to this.[22]

In 2011, Martin-Smith entered a boy band called, *The Mend*, into the X-factor. They were told by Gary Barlow to *"Get ready 'cos your lives are going to change forever."* However, they were then thrown off the show as the fact that they had an existing manager in Martin-Smith was against the show's regulations. Martin-Smith's anger with Simon Cowell was appeased when they were later allowed to appear on Britain's Got Talent.

COPYRIGHT IN PHOTOGRAPHY AND BREACH OF CONFIDENCE

THE SUN AND OASIS

On 16th April 1997, a photography session took place at the Stocks Country Club Hotel, Hertfordshire. The hotel was apparently a favourite of Keith Moon, the Who's drummer. Moon was well known for his erratic and destructive behaviour, and was rumoured to have once driven a Rolls Royce into a hotel swimming pool, although lead singer, Roger Daltrey, later stated that in fact he had driven a Chrysler Wimbledon into an ornamental pond.

The photos were being produced for the cover of Oasis's third album, *Be Here Now*. Originally, the plan had been to take four photos of different band members in different locations chosen by them, with Liam Gallagher appearing in each. Noel Gallagher wanted to be photographed in a tree, playing the guitar; Alan White wanted to be pictured in an East End pub; Paul "Guigsy" McGuigan's choice was a beach in St Lucia; and Paul "Bonehead" Arthurs suggested that he would be portrayed relaxing by a swimming pool at night, with a Rolls Royce submerged in it, in tribute to Keith Moon. However, this idea was abandoned as it was believed that it would not have the required impact.

Instead, a scene was devised by Noel Gallagher, lead guitarist of the band, incorporating one of the themes originally suggested. The photograph was set around the swimming pool, in which a white Rolls Royce was partially submerged. One member of the band was emerging from the pool and the other three were stood around it. A scooter and a range of random objects, selected from the BBC props store, were positioned around the pool.

A number of photographs were taken by the official photographer, Mr Michael Spencer Jones. The intention had apparently been to keep the photo-shoot a secret, with a limited number of people being aware of the arrangements. However, word clearly got out, as The Sun newspaper booked two rooms in the hotel, for the nights of 15th and 16th April, and contracted a freelance photographer, named Mr Seeburg, to stay at the hotel, and to try to take pictures of the scene. Mr Seeburg later claimed that another photographer, from the Daily Star, was also staying at the hotel, and that a number of the fans and also hotel staff watched the photo-shoot. Spencer Jones later described the session as *"chaotic"* partly due to the amount of alcohol which was consumed.

Mr Seeburg took a number of photos of the scene, one of which, he stated, was taken 15-20 feet to the left of the official photographer. This photo was published, along with two other photos of the scene, in the Sun, on 17th April, and again on 18th April. On the 19th April, the Sun offered readers the opportunity to purchase *"a glossy poster of The Sun's world exclusive of the new Oasis album shoot"* for the price of £1.99.

As a result of the publication of the photographs, and the offer of the poster, an application for an interlocutory injunction restraining publication was submitted against News Group Newspapers Limited by Oasis's UK record label, Creation Records Limited, alongside fellow plaintiffs, Noel Gallagher and Sony Music Entertainment Limited, (which owned 50% of Creation). Mr Justice Lloyd granted a temporary injunction on Monday 21st April, having heard the applicant's case only. On 25 April 1997, he heard from both parties in order to decide whether to extend the injunction until a full trial.

The applicants' case

The three plaintiffs put forward two arguments. First, they claimed that the photograph taken by Mr Seeberg, the Sun's contracted photographer, infringed their copyright. Alternatively, they claimed that its publication without their consent would be a breach of confidence, because of the circumstances in which it was obtained.[23]

The copyright argument

The plaintiffs' representative, Mr Merriman, commenced by putting forward the argument that the scene in the photograph (the band, the pool and the objects) was a copyrighted, dramatic or artistic work. The suggestion that it might be a "*dramatic*" work was quickly dismissed by Mr Justice Lloyd, on the grounds that it had "*no movement, story or action.*" However he gave more consideration to the alternative argument. This contended that the scene was an artistic work, as defined in *Section 4(1) or the Copyright, Designs and Patents Act 1988*:

> *In this Part "artistic work" means (a) a graphic work, photograph, sculpture or collage, irrespective of artistic quality, (b) a work of architecture being a building or a model for a building, or (c) a work of artistic craftsmanship.*

However, the Judge fairly quickly rejected this argument as well, observing:

> *I do not see how the process of assembling these disparate objects together with the members of the group can be regarded as having anything in common with sculpture or with artistic craftsmanship.*

He differentiated it from the case of *Shelley Films Limited v. Rex Features Ltd. [1994] EMLR 134*, where an unauthorised photograph of a film set, created for a film called "*Mary Shelley's Frankenstein*," was deemed to be a breach of copyright, on the grounds that the creation of the film set *did* involve craftsmanship. He also distinguished it from other artistic works which one might described as assemblies of disparate objects, on the grounds that such works were not ephemeral, unlike the objects assembled by Gallagher for the photography session, as these had been removed the following day.

Mr Merriman also offered a further copyright argument. In this, he claimed that Mr Seeberg's photograph was a copy of the official photograph. Unsurprisingly, this argument was also unsuccessful. As Mr Justice Lloyd pointed out, "*... it is a basic proposition of copyright law that two works created from a common source do not by reason of that fact involve copying one of the other, however similar they are.*" The only way in which such a claim would be successful were if Mr Seeberg had directly copied the photograph taken by the official photographer, rather than having taken his own photograph of the same scene. A further attempt to suggest that Noel Gallagher was the creator of Mr Seeburg's photograph because he had created the scene was also quickly rejected. In doing so, Mr Justice Lloyd made a definitive statement about the ownership of copyright in photographs:

It seems to me that ordinarily the creator of a photograph is the person who takes it. There may be cases where one person sets up the scene to be photographed (the position and angle of the camera and all necessary settings) and directs a second person to press the shutter at a moment chosen by the first, in which case it would be the first, not the second, who creates the photograph. There may also be cases of collaboration between the person behind the camera and one or more others in which the actual photographer has greater input, although no complete control of the creation of the photograph, in which case it would be the first, not the second, who creates the photograph. There may also be cases of collaboration between the person behind the camera and one or more others in which the actual photographer has greater input, although no complete control of the creation of the photograph, in which case it may be a work of joint creation and joint authorship.

Accordingly, Mr Justice Lloyd dismissed the claim that Mr Seeberg had infringed copyright. Some observers felt that the Judge's decision did not provide sufficient breadth in the definition of "*artistic work*". Others felt that the copyright case had no merit. Referring to the case in a later judgment in the House of Lords, Baroness Hale of Richmond expressed some disdain:

The most striking feature of the case, to my mind, is the lengths to which the record company's counsel went in seeking to establish an arguable case as to the infringement of some recognised intellectual property right [...] the barrel of intellectual property rights was thoroughly scraped.[24]

The case for breach of confidence

The Judge therefore moved on to consider the question of confidentiality. Putting forward a case for breach of confidence, Mr Merriman, on behalf of the plaintiffs, claimed that the photographs taken by Mr Seeburg were acquired:

in circumstances in which he must have realised that it was a breach of confidentiality to do so, or at least it would be such a breach to make the photograph available for publication

There was, however, conflict over the facts which the sides presented to the Judge in relation to the photo-shoot. Mr Seeburg's account indicated that there was a relatively relaxed atmosphere in the vicinity of the photo-shoot. He suggested that security was in place, but nevertheless members of the public were able to watch what was happening, talk to the band, and take photographs. He did not see anyone being asked what they were doing, and he was not asked either, even though he claimed that at one stage he was taking photographs just six feet from Mr Spencer Jones, the official photographer. He stated that at no point was he, or anyone else who was taking photographs, asked to stop.

The description of the event was somewhat different according to the plaintiffs. Mr Merriman contrasted Mr Seeburg's account with a comment in the Sun, which stated *"We got the shots despite a tight ring of security men and minders."* Further evidence was provided by an employee of the band's managers, named Mr McKinlay, and by Emma Greengrass, Marketing Manager for Creation Records. According to their account an area around the pool was roped off, but nevertheless about fifteen people did get access to the area. Some of them had cameras, and security guards were instructed to only allow them to take pictures of the band, not of the whole scene. They were unaware that Mr Seeburg was a freelance, professional photographer, and he had not been seen taking photographs. Mr McKinlay claimed that, had he been seen, then action would have been taken, with his film possibly being confiscated. He also claimed that other people had been prevented from taking photographs. Both Mr McKinlay and Ms Greengrass claimed that steps were taken to prevent photos being taken once the scene was ready for the official photographer. They suggested therefore that Mr Seeburg must have been aware that he would have been stopped if anyone had seen him, and he had therefore acted evasively and taken great steps to avoid being observed.

Mr Merriman referred to the case of *Shelley Films Limited v. Rex Features Ltd* (cited earlier) where a claim against a photographer who had surreptitiously taken photographs of the film set was successful on the basis of breach of confidence. There were some more important differences in the two cases, as, in the Shelley case, there were signs prohibiting photography, and the photographer had no legal entitlement to be in the location. Nevertheless, Mr Justice Lloyd saw a parallel between the cases.

He accepted that Mr Seeburg was entitled to be at the hotel, and that his presence around the photo-shoot was tolerated, and also that the taking of photographs was allowed before the official shoot began. However, he also accepted the plaintiffs' evidence that security was tightened once the shoot itself started, that the photographic record of the scene was intended to be confidential and that Mr Seeburg must have acted in an evasive manner in order to obtain his photographs.

The Judge also examined the potential damage which might be caused to each side by granting or not granting the injunction, and determined that, on balance, Oasis and their representatives had more to lose by publication, than the Sun had by not publishing. He therefore stated his decision:

> On that footing it seems to me that the plaintiffs do have a
> sufficiently arguable case for saying that the taking of the
> photograph and its publication is in breach of confidence and that
> future publication can be restrained by injunction at any rate until
> the image is fully released into the public domain, presumably on
> publication of the album, if it does come out with this cover.

In Para 291 of the House of Lords judgment referred to above, Baroness Hale of Richmond suggested that the defendant's representative may have missed a trick in their defence:

> In the Oasis case the defendants seem not to have relied on Lord
> Goff's second limiting principle (in Attorney-General v Guardian
> Newspapers Ltd No. 2 [1990] 1 AC 109, 282), that the law of
> confidence does not protect trivia. Photographs of a white Rolls
> Royce in a swimming pool may be thought to be a fairly trivial
> trade secret.

Conclusion and Epilogue

Be Here Now was released in the UK in August 1997. It sold 696,000 copies in the first week, making it the fastest-selling album in British history. The cover incorporated the photograph taken at the Stocks Country Club, and the date on the calendar shown on the cover was changed according to the release date in each region. Subsequent sales of the album were more disappointing, especially in the US, and the album is now viewed as marking the beginning of the decline of "Britpop." In September 2012, Noel Gallagher stated in an interview in NME that he did not want to make an album as bad as "*Be Here Now*", describing it as:

> *the sound of a bunch of guys, on coke, in the studio, not giving a fuck. All the songs are really long and all the lyrics are shit and for every millisecond Liam is not saying a word, there's a fucking guitar riff in there in a Wayne's World style.*

The album cover itself is included in Virgin Media's list of the 20 most pretentious album covers.

In 1997 and 1998 Oasis undertook an 85-date tour, which used a stage set which included a Rolls Royce, an over-sized telephone box, and other items from the *Be Here Now* album cover.

Michael Spencer Jones continued his career as a successful freelance photographer, working with a number of bands including The Verve.

The ruling made by Mr Justice Lloyd came under further discussion in 2012. The case of *Temple Island Collection Limited v New English Teas Limited [2012] EWPCC 1* related to a photograph of a red London bus crossing Westminster Bridge, created by Temple Island Collection. The Houses of Parliament were shown in the background, which was all monochrome.

New English Teas had originally used the photograph without permission, but had withdrawn its use following action from Temple Island. It then used computer software to recreate the scene, including the red London bus, and bridge and Houses of Parliament in monochrome, albeit seen from a slightly different angle. This kind of recreation would, on the surface, appear to be acceptable within copyright law, as it is no more than a computerised version of what Mr Seeburg did at the Stocks Hotel. However, Mr Justice Birss examined a range of factors, including the angle of the shot, lighting, exposure and effects, and ruled that New English teas *had* infringed the copyright in the original photograph, because they had copied a substantial part of the composition of the original image. The decision drew much comment about the implications for copyright protection of photographs. See, for example, the 1709 Blog[25], and Walker Morris[26].

Jeremy Grice

FILM, DANCE AND COPYRIGHT ISSUES

GUINNESS

On 16 May 1994 a TV and Cinema commercial named *Anticipation* was shown for the first time in the Republic of Ireland and Northern Ireland, promoting Guinness Stout. Later that year it was also shown in England and Wales, with a minor difference in that an English-shaped, rather than Irish-shaped, pint glass was used.

The commercial featured an actor called Joseph McKinney who played a man who was waiting somewhat impatiently for his pint of Guinness to settle so that he can drink it. (For those unfamiliar with the drink, official advice from the Guinness company is that a pint should be poured in two stages, with the entire process taking 119.53 seconds). During his wait, the man carries out a quirky dance, observed by the barman. Finally, he gets the satisfaction of drinking his pint (though interestingly his wait in the commercial was only 60, not 119.53, seconds) The commercial used a "jump-cutting" technique so that the dancing man appeared to be performing a series of jerky movements, which would not have been possible in a real, live performance.

The commercial was apparently inspired from two sources. The first was a scene in *The Snapper* by Roddy Doyle, when a man who is impatient to celebrate the birth of his grandchild, nevertheless has to wait for his Guinness to settle before his celebration can begin. The second inspiration was a short film called *Joy*, which was included in a showreel produced by a film director called Mehdi Norowzian. The showreel had been distributed to a number of companies to promote Norowzian's work. One of the companies which received the showreel was an Irish organisation called Arks, which had been appointed by Guinness (Ireland) Limited as their advertising agent.

Arks approached Norowzian and invited him to direct their Guinness commercial. However he turned them down as he believed that they simply wanted to remake *Joy* with a beer glass superimposed, and felt that "*it would have involved no creativity on my part.*" In his response to their request, he suggested that they "*should stay well way from Joy.*"

Arks therefore engaged another director, called Ritchie Smyth, and a new storyboard was created, which, Arks considered, was more remote from *Joy*. They did suggest that Smyth utilised the jump cutting techniques, though these were reasonably widely used within the film industry.

After seeing the commercial in July 1994, Mr Norowzian instructed solicitors to write to Arks alleging breach of copyright and threatening legal proceedings. Over the next two to three years there was further correspondence from different solicitors acting for Mr Norowzian. On one occasion, he offered to settle if Arks paid him £200,000 plus costs. This offer did appear to contradict later statements from him that he was undertaking action as a point of principle rather than for financial reasons. Finally, on 17 March 1997 he issued a writ against Arks Limited, Guinness Brewing Worldwide Limited and Guinness PLC, alleging infringement of copyright and "passing off." The action for "passing off" was abandoned before the case reached court. They also withdrew the claim against Guinness PLC during the court case itself.

The initial court case

Norowozian's claim was that his film, *Joy*, was a dramatic work as defined within the *Copyright, Designs and Patents Act 1988*, and that his rights as author had been infringed because *Anticipation*

74

included a copy of a substantial part of that work. His claim referred, inter alia, to Section 3 of the Act, which provides a definition of a *"dramatic work"* as one which *"includes a work of dance or mime"*. The court case took place on 17 July 1998, before Mr Justice Rattee. Extracts below are from the court transcript *Norowzian v Arks Limited and Others [1998] EWHX 315.*

Mr Justice Rattee made it clear that he needed to be satisfied on two issues if Mr Norowzian's claim for copyright infringement were to be satisfied:

> *(a) that his film "Joy" does indeed constitute or comprise a "dramatic work" and*

> *(b) that "Anticipation" is, or includes, a copy of a substantial part of that dramatic work*

In examining the first of these factors, Mr Justice Rattee reasoned that a film could be a *recording* of a dramatic work, but could not, in itself, be a dramatic work. He appeared to dismiss this possibility quite quickly; in doing so he seemed partly to have been influenced by the submission of Mr Floyd, Norowzian's representative, who had put no real case forward in this respect, observing *"Joy is clearly a work of dance and mime which has been recorded on film."*

The Judge then went on to conclude that *"Joy"* was *not* a recording of a dramatic work, because the final product was so different to the actual performance which took place on account of the editing techniques which were employed. He observed that if a work were to be protected as a *"dramatic work"* then it needed to be capable of physical performance, noting that, whilst impressive, this was not the case with *"Joy"*:

The result is striking, but unreal. No human performer could have performed the routine displayed by the film. It would be a physical impossibility.

An alternative approach might have been to suggest that *"Joy"* would be protected under *Section (1)(1)(b) of the Copyright, Designs and Patents Act* which states directly that Copyright is a property right which subsists in films. Indeed this was an initial claim put forward by Mr Norowzian, however the claim was struck out by the court in December 1997 since such infringement requires wholesale copying of the subject matter of the film, and this had clearly not occurred.

Mr Floyd, Norowzian's representative, suggested that this interpretation left a serious gap in the protection provided by the 1988 Act, with the originality of film-makers left unprotected. The Judge's response was that it was not open to him to stretch the meaning of *"dramatic work"* in order to provide such protection.

However, he then went on to examine the second question of whether or not *Anticipation* was a copy of *Joy*, in case a subsequent court found that he had erred in his conclusion that it was not entitled to copyright protection. In assessing the case the Judge described how *Anticipation* had been created, referring to evidence which highlighted how *Joy* had been used as a source, which had then been developed by the choreographer and main character. He took evidence from an independent expert choreographer, Miss Eyles, who observed:

I believe that any similarities which do exist between Joy and Anticipation lie principally in the visual impact of the two works; an impact which is achieved by camera positions and filming, cutting and editing techniques. […] In terms of performance, in my opinion, the dramatic work entitled Anticipation does not replicate any significant elements of the dramatic work entitled Joy.

Nevertheless, a witness statement from Joseph McKinney, the actor who played the main character, explained that he had been encouraged to *"imitate, emulate and expand upon 'Joy'"*. In particular, he commented:

> *There is no doubt in my mind that 'Joy' was central to the advertisement and that this was understood throughout by Ritchie Smith [sic], Gary Lowe, the choreographer and myself.*

Another choreographer, called by Mr Norowzian, did identify a *"long list of alleged similarities"* between the two films however the Judge was not impressed by them, commenting:

> *some were only a fraction of a second in length, and some so short that they could only be perceived by means of a video recorder set to show the films in very slow motion, so that they would have been invisible to anyone watching the films at normal viewing speed.*

The Judge appeared to prefer the evidence of his own viewing of the films, and furthermore criticized the provision of expert evidence as a waste of time and money. He accepted some similarities in some dance movements, but highlighted differences in the setting, subject matter, number of characters and overall substance. He reached the conclusion that whilst *"Anticipation"* used similar filming and editing techniques to *"Joy"*, it did not copy a substantial part of it.

> *I am satisfied that Joy provided Arks with an idea which was developed into Anticipation by Mr Smyth by the use of similar filming techniques to those used by Mr Norowzian in Joy. It seems to me clear that Joy was used by Arks and Mr Smyth as a point of reference in the production of Anticipation. But, in my judgment, it is impossible to say that Anticipation reproduces a substantial part of the subject matter of Joy, or, therefore of any dramatic work that might be comprised in Joy.*

The appeal

Mr Norowzian lodged an appeal against the judgment, claiming that *Joy* itself should have been accepted as a dramatic work, and asserting again that *Anticipation* had copied a substantial part of *Joy*. The Appeal was heard on 4 November 1999, before Lord Justice Nourse, Lord Justice Brooke and Lord Justice Buxton.[27]

In the appeal, Mr Norowzian's new representative, a Mr Arnold, based the first part of his case on a claim that *Joy* itself was a dramatic work. In the initial court case, this idea had been dismissed by Mr Justice Rattee. Lord Justice Nourse expressed the view that this dismissal had been influenced by the fact that the representative for Mr Norowzian in the original case, Mr Floyd, had not really presented a case for it, instead stating that "*Joy is clearly a work of dance and mime which has been recorded on film.*" A dispute ensued as to whether the plaintiff should, on appeal, be allowed to submit an argument which had not been put forward in the original case, with the defendants claiming that, had it been put forward, then they would have submitted a defence to it.

Nevertheless, Lord Nourse allowed the submission. He accepted Mr Justice Rattee's logic that *Joy* could not be a recording of a dramatic work because the dance could not be performed as shown. However, he accepted the submission within the appeal that it could be a dramatic work in itself; effectively he regarded the showing of the film to an audience as satisfying the requirement of it being capable of being performed.

> *In my judgment a film can be a dramatic work for the purposes of the 1988 Act. [...] A film will often, though not always, be a work of action and it is capable of being performed before an audience. It can therefore fall within the expression "dramatic work" in section 1(1)(a) and I disagree with the Judge's reasons for excluding it.*

The other two members of the Appeal Court panel agreed with this. Lord Buxton further suggested that the Court would be required to include films within the protection provided by the *Copyright, Designs and Patents Act 1988* as part of the UK's obligations under the Berne Convention on copyright:

> *if the 1988 Act is to be interpreted consistently with this country's international obligations under the Convention, the cinematographic works referred to in the Convention have all to be included within the Act's category of dramatic works: even in cases where the natural meaning of "dramatic work" does not or might not embrace the particular film in question.*

Having accepted that *Joy* was entitled to protection, the Appeal Panel then examined the question of whether the defendants had copied a substantial part of it when they produced *Anticipation*. In this area, there was unanimity, with the Appeal Judges concurring wholly with Mr Justice Rattee:

> *I think it is impossible to say that Anticipation is or includes a copy of a substantial part of Joy. As the Judge recognised, the highest it can be put in favour of the claimant is that there is a striking similarity between the filming and editing styles and techniques used by the respective directors of the two films. But no copyright subsists in mere style or technique.*

As a result, the appeal was dismissed, with Mr Norowzian liable for costs.

Analysis and Epilogue

For Mr Norowzian there was nothing to be gained from the partial success of the Appeal, but from a wider perspective there certainly were benefits. The original ruling by Mr Justice Rattee had attracted widespread comment. Margaret Briffa of London-based Briffa & Co, who represented Mr Norowzian in the case, felt that it was bad news all round, as it meant that film directors would have no real protection for the work they created, apart from protection for direct copying of the whole work. She observed that the decision would *"deal a major blow to advertising agencies, film directors and all involved in film and video work."*

Similarly, an article in PR Week, in July 1998, commented:

The ruling, if upheld, establishes two things, neither of which is to do with the protection of ideas. Firstly, finished (i.e. edited) films are not protected from anything but mechanical copying. Secondly, in British law, the style of a film is distinct from its content. So the work of those in charge of the style (directors) is exempt from copyright, while the work of those in charge of content (writers) is protected.

It suggested that the law need to be changed or re-interpreted, and that whilst it was good news for those who wanted to copy other people's work, it was not so good for those who produced creative and innovative films.

An article in The Times, on 25 August 1998, agreed with this opinion:

Mr Justice Rattee stated that in order for films like Joy to be protected, there would need to be an extension of the 1988 legislation. That is surely correct. As we move into the next millennium, the artistry and sophistication of professional film-making is, many would argue, just as challenging, creative and technical a business as other art forms like poetry or the short-story. Why should what a former Master of the Rolls, Lord Greene, once referred to as 'the fruit of the brains, skill, imagination, and taste' of particular artists, like those who direct a short film, be less protected than those which write a drama?

In the event, there was no need for new legislation, as the Appeal judgment effectively provided double protection for films, first against whole-scale piracy, and secondly as a dramatic work. In doing so it also ensured protection for cartoons and other filmed activities which were not capable of physical performance.

Anticipation won advertising awards for editing and creativity in 1995. Actor Joe McKinney spent two years on a European tour promoting Guinness, before giving up alcohol in 1997 and focusing on his acting career. He took many parts in the USA where he was less recognised as the *"dancing Guinness man"*. *Anticipation* was shown on TV again in 2004 and 2009, as part of a revival of classic Guinness advertisements. It was also mimicked in an advert, called *Eskimo*, which promoted ice-cold Guinness. Mehdi Norowzian went on to direct two films: *Killing Joe* (1999), starring Daniel Bliss and *Leo* (2002) starring Joseph Fiennes and Elizabeth Shue.

A similar dispute took place in 2003 when the advertisement *"Cog"* appeared on TV, promoting Honda cars. The advertising agency responsible for it received correspondence from Peter Fischli and David Weiss, creators of the 1987 film *Der Lauf Der Dinge*, highlighting similarities between the film and the advertisement. The two creators had apparently refused several requests to base advertisements on their film and stated that they would have refused Honda permission, had they been asked. Furthermore the advertising agency responsible admitted that the film was an inspiration for the advertisement, and that they had passed copies of it to their script-writers. In the event, however, the dispute did not reach court.

Jeremy Grice

COPYRIGHT ISSUES AND CONTRACTS

SPANDAU BALLET

The journey which eventually led to the formation of Spandau Ballet began in North London in 1976, when Gary Kemp and Steve Norman formed a band called *"The Cut."* School friends Tony Hadley and John Keeble joined them, along with Gary Kemp's brother, Martin, thereby establishing the line-up which would take them successfully through the 1980s. A further school friend, Steve Dagger, became their manager. Allegedly inspired by some graffiti on the wall of a Berlin nightclub, they acquired the name *"Spandau Ballet"*. In October 1980, following keen interest from a number of record companies, they signed with Chrysalis Records, receiving a record advance payment of £85,000, despite the fact that, at the time, they had only played eight live gigs.

Over the next nine years, the band released six albums, two compilations, and 23 singles. They won a BRIT Award in 1984. Their third album, *True,* released in 1983, topped the album charts in the UK and in New Zealand. It contained the band's most successful singles, *Gold,* which reached number 2 in the UK Charts and *True,* which reached Number One in the UK and Number 4 in the USA.

The final album of their initial existence, *Heart Like a Sky,* was released in 1989, by which time they had changed record companies to CBS, following a legal case against Chrysalis, who they accused of not promoting the band effectively in the USA. *Heart Like a Sky* did not achieve the success of previous releases, reaching number 31 in the UK Charts, but not being released in the USA. They toured to promote the album, with a final performance in Edinburgh on 6 March 1990. Following that the band did not perform together until they reunited in 2009.

Following their break up, a dispute arose over distribution of income from the band's activities, resulting in a court case, with Gary Kemp and *"Reformation"*, a company owned by him, as defendants, and Tony Hadley, John Keeble and Steve Norman as plaintiffs (or "complainants/claimants"). Gary's brother, Martin, remained on the sidelines.

Spandau Ballet's popularity could perhaps be measured by the fact that even the lead Judge in the case, Mr Justice Park, was familiar with their music, commenting in his written transcript:

> *Spandau Ballet was not just commercially successful. It was highly regarded during its years of success by many informed and critical observers of the popular music world.* [28]

Legal structure

Spandau Ballet began life as a partnership, albeit without any written partnership agreement. However, they followed legal advice that they should create a corporate structure, and this was completed prior to signing their recording contract with Chrysalis. The band purchased a company called *Marbelow Limited*. The shares were equally owned by the five band members and their manager, and all six of them were directors. The five band members had employment agreements to provide *Marbelow* exclusively with their recording and performance services. Importantly, song-writing and composing services were specifically *excluded* from the employment agreements.

A further company was set up to handle income from song-writing and composing. This company was called *Reformation Limited* and was owned solely by Gary Kemp, who, at the time, was regarded as the song-writer. Steve Dagger was also a Director of *Reformation*, but owned no shares.

Sources of Income

The dispute between the members of Spandau Ballet revolved around one specific income stream resulting from the band's activities, traditionally referred to as *"Publishing income"*. It is essential to understand the difference between the income streams generated by bands such as Spandau Ballet before examining the dispute in detail. Mr Justice Park was obviously aware of the importance of this, and gave a thorough and accurate explanation of these income streams in the transcript of his judgment. The key points are summarised below.

There are varying sources of income for a band:

- Recording income

- Publishing income

- Income from live performances

- Merchandising Income

Income from the latter two sources is not relevant to the case and would normally be split equally between the members of the band. Income from those sources is also likely to dry up once the band stops working together. Income from recording and publishing is central to the case; to help to understand these it is best to start by considering the question of copyright.

Copyright in musical works, literary works and recorded performances

When a song is written and recorded, a number of copyrights are created:

- Copyright in the music – the *"musical work"*

- Copyright in the lyrics – the *"literary work"*

- Copyright in the performance of the song (as recorded)

The first two of the above copyrights are owned initially by the composer and the writer (though these may be the same person). If the composer and writer are employed to compose and/or write, then copyright belongs to their employer. In the case of Spandau Ballet it was originally assumed (until the court case) that Gary Kemp was composer of the music and the writer of the lyrics. He was employed as composer and writer by *Reformation* for all of the band's albums except the first, but he also assigned the ownership of the copyrights in the musical and literary works on the first album to *Reformation*.

The ownership of the copyright in Spandau Ballet's *recorded* performances would initially have vested in the band as performers. However, as is normal in the recording industry, ownership of the copyright in the recording was transferred as part of the contractual agreement with Chrysalis (for the first four albums and three subsequent compilations) and with CBS (for the final two albums). So *Reformation* owned copyright in the musical and literary works, and Chrysalis or CBS owned copyright in the recordings.

Income from Recorded Performances

Different flows of income emanate from recorded performances:

- *"Publishing income"* results from the copyright in the music and lyrics of the song.

- *"Recording income"* results from the artists' performances in making the recordings of the songs.

Publishing income is due to the owner of the copyright in the music and lyrics. It is produced from a range of sources:

- Sales of sheet music (generally minimal).

- Licensing third parties to give live performances.

- *"Mechanical royalties"* in recordings. These are paid by the record company according to the number of CDs etc. which have been produced, in return for a license from the copyright owner to record the material. In the 1980s they were calculated at 6.25% of the retail selling price.

- Performing royalties in the recording, payable when a record is performed in public. This would cover performances on the radio, in public areas and so on, usually licensed through the Performing Rights Society (PRS). These may be due internationally as well as nationally, and the income flow for a successful band such as Spandau Ballet may well continue after the band has stopped recording and touring, if their music continues to be played publicly in a widespread manner.

- *"Synchronisation"* arrangements, whereby the music is utilised in films, on TV, in adverts or in games. This is an area which has become much more important in recent years than it was during the 80s.

For an excellent explanation of the potential income from publishing, visit the blog *WTF is Music Publishing?* by Sentric Music.[29]

Recording Income is due to the performers (or their employers). The members of Spandau Ballet were employed by *Marbelow* for their recording services. Accordingly recording royalties would have been paid by Chrysalis/CBS to the company, which would then have paid salaries and bonuses to the band members (having first deducted operating expenses). Normally a recording contract will be set up so that the record company pays an up-front, non-returnable advance to the performers. Performers are due a percentage of all income from sales (royalties). These are credited against the initial lump sum until the point at which royalties exceed it; this is known as *recoupment*. From then on royalties are paid to the performers (or their representatives).

As with income streams from live performances and merchandising, recording income would tend to dry up once a band had split up. Income from publishing would be much more likely to continue (assuming the band's recordings continue to be played in public, used on TV etc.) In the case of Spandau Ballet, live performance and recording income would be passed to *Marbelow*, to be then split six ways, between the five band members and the manager. Publishing income belonged solely to Gary Kemp/*Reformation* (although as we will see later, for some time he did share that income.) The diagram below illustrates the income split.

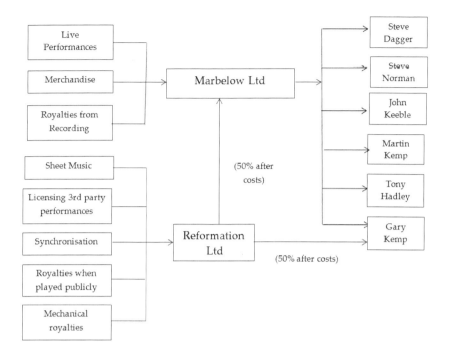

The dispute

The dispute between Gary Kemp and the other members of Spandau Ballet centred on the distribution of publishing income. As discussed above, publishing income was distributed through *Reformation Limited*, a company wholly owned by Gary Kemp, who was, at the time, regarded as the songwriter and composer. However, for a period of seven years from 1981 onwards, payments were made from *Reformation* to *Marbelow Limited* (the company owned by the five members of Spandau Ballet and their manager). The payments were made on an on-going basis during the financial year, and at the end of the year an adjustment was made so that the amount paid equated to approximately half of *Reformation's* profits (being Publishing Income less operating expenses). The amounts were identified in *Reformation's* accounts as *"Band Support."* The matching income receipts were shown in *Marbelow's* accounts as *"Promotional Fee."*

Gary Kemp decided to stop making the payments as from 31 December 1987. The total paid from *Reformation* to *Marbelow* in the previous seven years amounted to more than £1.8m. Mr Justice Park estimated that, had the payments continued from 1988 until the time of the court case, then *Reformation* would have paid *Marbelow* between £1.5m and £2m more. Half of that figure would have been due to the plaintiffs (with the other half belonging to Gary Kemp, Martin Kemp and Steve Dagger). That estimate certainly demonstrates the value of publishing income, and how it continued beyond the life of the band.

Tony Hadley, Steve Norman and John Keeble put forward two separate rationales to support their case that the payments from *Reformation* should not have stopped.

First, they claimed that there was an implied contract between *Reformation* and *Marbelow*, and that Gary Kemp's action in stopping the payments was a breach of contract. Furthermore they claimed that Kemp had not informed them that the payments had stopped, suggesting that this was the reason why they had taken so long to bring the case to court.

Their second claim was put forward in case the contractual claim was unsuccessful, and argued that they were joint copyright owners of the musical works (not the lyrics), and they were therefore entitled to a part share of all publishing income.

The contractual claim

Mr Justice Park succinctly summarised the questions to be considered in relation to the contractual claim:

Was there, as the plaintiffs say, an agreement reached in oral discussions under which Gary Kemp was legally bound to make to the other members of the band and to Mr Dagger payments of shares of his publishing income? Or was there, as the defendants

say, a unilateral decision reached by Mr Kemp that, without any
legally binding agreement, he would for the time being pay a share
of his publishing income to the band?

In the event that a contractually binding verbal agreement had been made, then 50% of publishing income should have gone to Gary Kemp, and 50% gone to *Marbelow*. The latter 50% would then be split equally between the five band members and their manager. As a result, Gary Kemp would receive 7/12 of the income, and the other band members (and the manager) would receive 1/12 each.

The plaintiffs explained how publishing income was something they had discussed during the early days of the band, when they were starting to become successful, but further discussion had been delayed until the recording contract was in place. Eventually discussions had culminated in the agreement to share the publishing income. They were unable, however, as Mr Justice Park put it, to identify *"specific meetings in specific places where these matters were agreed, or give evidence about who said precisely what to whom."* They believed, however, that the original agreement had been to pay these amounts directly to band members, and then this changed to Marbelow, once the company had been set up.

The defendants (Gary Kemp and Reformation) had a different recollection of events. Evidence to support their case was provided by Mr Kemp himself, and by Steve Dagger, who, as the band's manager, was deeply involved in the conversations which took place during the band's early days.

Both Gary Kemp and Steve Dagger agreed with the plaintiffs' account of the early days of the band, with much time spent together, and many conversations taking place between them. However they did not agree that publishing income had been a topic of conversation. They explained that they had had meetings with publishing companies to find out more about the industry, but without any intention to sign a publishing deal.

The main disparity between the accounts given by the defendants and the plaintiffs, however, was that Kemp and Dagger denied that any agreement had been made to share publishing income with the other members of the band, either generally, or in the specific proportions laid out by the plaintiffs. The obvious question raised by the denial was why payments were being made from *Reformation* to *Marbelow*.

Gary Kemp claimed that the decision to share the publishing income with the other members of the band was a unilateral one, motivated by several factors.

The first of these followed a conversation with a record producer, Richard Burgess, who had alerted Kemp to the division which occurred sometimes in a band between the songwriter(s) and the rest of the band, because of the imbalance in income caused by the size of the income stream from publishing. Burgess was also in a band, and had resolved the issue by giving a 50% interest in copyrights to the other band members.

Kemp was also aware that the expenses which Spandau Ballet incurred, paid by *Marbelow*, were high and would not necessarily be covered by the recording royalties. Furthermore, he accepted that publishing income was enhanced by the fact that the songs were performed and recorded by the band.

Having made the decision, Kemp was unclear about how it had been communicated to the rest of the band, though he believed it was in January 1981. Steve Dagger recalled his relief on being advised by Kemp of the decision, as he had been worried about the high running expenses of *Marbelow*. Kemp did state, however, that, contrary to the plaintiffs' evidence, there had never been a stage when payments were to be made directly to band members, as, by the time he decided to make the payments, *Marbelow* was already in existence. Consistent with this, he claimed never to have thought in terms of the other band members getting a 1/12 each; rather he was thinking in terms of a 50/50 split between himself and *Marbelow*. Whilst this effectively would be the same, it did confirm that, in Kemp's belief, the decision did not take place until *Marbelow* and *Reformation* were set up. He further believed that the decision was a unilateral and non-binding one, which he was free to revoke whenever he wanted to.

The contractual claim - the Judgment

Mr Justice Park provided two rationales for his decision. The first of these was based on his interpretation of the facts of the case which had been presented to him. The second was based on his interpretation of the law of contract as it applied to the case. The two rationales are described separately below.

Contractual claim – Judgment on the facts

The difficulty for the Judge when examining the facts lay in the substantial variations between the explanation given by the defendants for the payments being made by *Reformation* to *Marbelow* and the explanation given by the plaintiffs. Of course, such variations are not unusual in a case that has reached court. However it means that, to make judgment, the Judge needed to determine which account he believed. In some cases, this may not be difficult because one set of witnesses is far more credible than the other. However, as the Judge observed, this was not the situation in this case:

> *[The plaintiffs] were honest, able and engaging witnesses. I am sure that the evidence which they gave to me of the events of 1980 and 1981 consisted of sincere accounts of how they remember those events to have been. The problem is that the same is true of the*

accounts given to me by Gary Kemp and Mr Dagger, both of whom were, in my opinion, every bit as impressive witnesses as the plaintiffs.

Having stated the problem which he faced, Mr Justice Park then went on how to describe how he would reach a decision by examining the *"quality"* of the evidence, in order to determine which account was more likely to have been true, particularly taking into account independent witnesses who had less to gain from the case, and trying to assess which witnesses would have been more likely to have an accurate recollection of matters. However, importantly, he emphasised that it was for the plaintiffs to *prove* their case. This being a civil case, the burden of proof was on the *"balance of probabilities"*, not *"beyond reasonable doubt"*, but as he made clear: *"if the judge feels that the case is evenly balanced the plaintiff loses."*

In looking for independent witnesses the Judge considered a range of individuals. His evaluation of their evidence is described below.

Steve Dagger

As band manager Dagger clearly was involved in the majority of conversations and negotiations. He also would be likely to have a more in-depth understanding of the income streams available to the band, and a responsibility for managing them, on behalf of *all* members of the band.

As owner of a sixth of *Marbelow*, he might be said to have a vested interest in the plaintiffs' case, as he would benefit if *Reformation* were ordered to pay publishing income to *Marbelow*. However, this would be partially counteracted by the fact that he was Gary Kemp's manager, and would lose commission on Kemp's income.

The Judge appeared to be impressed by Dagger, describing him as *"a capable and conscientious manager"* and *"gifted with an extensive and retentive memory."* Conversely, the plaintiffs' representative, Mr Sutcliffe, had clearly tried to discredit Steve Dagger during the trial, describing him as an unreliable witness who was overly assertive, and suggesting that he was presenting his evidence in a manner which would suit Gary Kemp. It would appear from the Judge's comments that such attempts were counter-productive.

Overall, Steve Dagger's evidence confirmed that, from his recollection, any agreement to share publishing income was voluntary, not contractual, and that had it been otherwise, then he would have been aware of it:

> *I know that that was never ever agreed or said by anybody in my presence. Or, as I was the manager of the group at the time and speaking to everybody on a daily basis, if such an agreement had existed I would certainly have known about it.*

Mr Brian Carr

Carr was Spandau Ballet's solicitor, and had been involved with the band since their earliest days, providing them with advice on how to structure their activities, and on achieving a recording contract. As a solicitor, he was in the habit of making attendance notes of conversations and meetings, and he had a strong belief that all agreements between the band members should be documented. There were several key aspects to Carr's evidence.

He recalled that, in the early days of the band, the focus was very much on sorting out the record deal, observing, *"I think it was most unlikely that I would be talking about publishing."*

He had an attendance note of the meeting of 10 October 1980, at which the recording contract with Chrysalis was signed. The note made no reference to any discussion about publishing income, even though the plaintiffs had claimed that it had been the subject of discussion. He also made an attendance note of a meeting on 2 February 1981, which included the statement:

Discussing publishing arrangements. In relation to Gary's songs, he was prepared to pass over to other members of the Group 5/12 keeping to himself 7/12.

He had assumed prior to this meeting that the band wrote the music together. On discovering that Kemp was the sole composer and writer he advised him to establish *Reformation* with himself as sole shareholder. Whilst not recalling details of the meeting, he was clear that, had he been told that there was to be a legally binding agreement to share the publishing income, then he would have strongly advised that it be documented formally. He commented *"it was asking for trouble for such rights and obligations to be left unrecorded, in particular when they were said to arise from internal discussions."*

The plaintiffs' representative, Mr Sutcliffe, focused particularly on the reference to 5/12 and 7/12 in Carr's attendance note. He maintained that this confirmed his clients' claim that they had each been promised 1/12 of the publishing income. Neither Gary Kemp nor Carr could remember whether the words were Kemp's, or whether they were Carr's interpretation of what he had said. Steve Dagger could not remember the exact words either. In his original statement, he referred to 5/12ths and 7/12ths, but he later revised that to simply refer to proportions, claiming that he had only referred to the exact fractions after reading the attendance notes. Mr Sutcliffe attempted to use this change as evidence of Dagger modifying the evidence in a suspicious and unsatisfactory manner, but he failed to persuade the Judge. Indeed the Judge felt that a more important assumption could be drawn from Carr's evidence:

The most important conclusion [...] is that, shortly after the decision about payments of publishing income had been made, Mr Kemp and Mr Dagger told Mr Carr about it. The basis on which they described it was that the payments were voluntary and unilateral on Mr Kemp's part. I go further and say, not just that that is what they told Mr Carr, but also that that is what they themselves believed.

The Judge was particularly persuaded by the use of the phrase *"he (Gary) was prepared to share"*, which he felt indicated the voluntary nature of the arrangement.

Miss Jackie Vickers

Jackie Vickers was Steve Dagger's assistant. She was keen to be impartial in the dispute, referring to all members of the band (and their families) as friends as well as work colleagues. She had worked as book-keeper for *Marbelow* and *Reformation* since 1982, and had dealt with payments from *Reformation* to *Marbelow*. When she asked about the nature of the payments, she was told by Steve Dagger that they were voluntary and informal payments, which Gary Kemp could stop at any time if she wanted to.

The Judge placed much weight on her explanation, because he concluded that, even if Mr Sutcliffe were tailoring evidence during the court case, he was unlikely to have been doing so in 1982 when discussing the matter with the company book-keeper.

Accounting and tax advisers

In a similar manner, the accountants for *Reformation* and *Marbelow* were advised by Steve Dagger about the payments from *Reformation* to *Marbelow*. Their evidence was that they had been told that the payments were voluntary contributions to the running costs of *Marbelow*, which were made at Kemp's discretion, and that he could halt them should he want to do so.

Furthermore, a tax specialist who reviewed the arrangement advised Dagger that, although the payments were voluntary, they could still be treated as tax-deductible because there was a commercial rationale behind them.

Jess Bailey

Jess Bailey was a keyboard player, who had been at school with Steve Dagger and four of the band members, and who played on the band's second and third albums. He recalled Dagger telling him about the arrangement to share the income, in the context of it being *"a generous and gratuitous gesture"* by Kemp. Again, the Judge placed weight on his evidence being an account of how Steve Dagger described the arrangement at a time when there was no motivation for him to tailor his evidence.

Evidence from the Band themselves

It is clear that the Judge felt that the evidence from the independent witnesses favoured the defendants. As highlighted earlier, he saw all the band members as being honest and sincere in their evidence. Nevertheless, he assessed the evidence given by each band member and its possible accuracy.

He felt that Gary Kemp was much more likely than the plaintiffs to have put thought into the nature of the arrangement, and was, as a result, more likely to have remembered how it was set up:

Mr Kemp was deciding whether to part with half of what he knew could turn into a substantial stream of income. That is not something which anyone would do without careful thought, and Mr Kemp's evidence, which could not realistically be doubted, is that he did think about it carefully and for some time. That being so I think that there is good reason to believe that he will remember, not just the decision in itself, but also the basis (unilateral decision or binding contract?) on which he regarded himself as making it.

He also assessed which of the two versions of events was more likely to have been the correct one. The plaintiffs' case was that a legal binding arrangement was more likely as that was the only way to avoid dissent and ill-feeling within the band over an unequal distribution of income. The defendants' case was that a voluntary, non-binding agreement would achieve the same result, and that was what had been set up. The Judge was of the same opinion:

In my view it is at least as likely that Gary Kemp would only be willing to make the payments if they were voluntary, so that he could discontinue them in future circumstances, as that he would want to bind himself contractually to make them in perpetuity.

Mr Justice Park's final conclusion therefore, having examined the facts of the case, was that the plaintiffs had failed to satisfy him that on the balance of probabilities there was a binding, oral agreement to share publishing income. Accordingly, Gary Kemp was free to halt the payments whenever he wanted to.

The contractual claim - Judgment on the law

Having examined the facts to make a judgment about the contractual claim, the Judge examined matters to determine whether plaintiffs could establish that a binding contractual agreement had been formed in line with the principles of the law of contract.

There is, of course, no obligation for a contract to be written for it to be binding on the parties, but there are four standard requirements which need to be satisfied to demonstrate that a contract has been formed:

- There must have been an offer.

- The parties must have had an intention to create legal relations.

- There must have been a clear acceptance of the offer.

- Consideration (or something of value) must have been exchanged between the parties.

In analysing the Spandau Ballet case, Mr Justice Park added another requirement:

> *If the terms of the offer are uncertain, the uncertainties must not be so great as to negate the existence of a binding contract.*

He then considered each step in turn.

Offer

Mr Sutcliffe tried to build a case that an offer had been made by Gary Kemp, even though he claimed that he did not mean to do so, and even though the plaintiffs could not remember when or where it was made. However, Mr Justice Park did not accept the argument, as he could find no evidence to back it up.

> *In this case it is not possible to consider objectively what Mr Kemp said. No one can tell me what it was, when and where he said it, or put it in the context of an entire conversation.*

As a result he concluded:

> *I am not satisfied on the balance of probabilities that Gary Kemp made to the plaintiffs a contractual offer to pay to them shares of his publishing income.*

Intention

He next examined the question of whether there was an intention to create legal relations. The strongest point which Mr Sutcliffe could put forward in this respect was that, generally, arrangements made within a business relationship are assumed by courts to have been put into place with an intention to create legal relations. However, set against that was the fact that the band members were friends from a long-time back so their relationship was one of friendship as well as business. Many of the statements made during the trial suggested that Gary Kemp had been made the payments from *Reformation* to *Marbelow* in the spirit of that friendship. Furthermore, in their evidence, Steve Dagger and Gary Kemp had demonstrated that, at the time the payments were being made, *and* at the time of the court case, they had no intention to create legal relations. As a result, the Judge stated that he was not persuaded that the decision to share publishing income was undertaken with an intention to create legal relations.

Acceptance

Unsurprisingly, given that the Judge could find no evidence of a contractual offer, he also could find no evidence that the plaintiffs had accepted an offer. His interpretation was that Gary Kemp had advised them of what he planned to do, and they agreed with it.

I cannot see in this anything more than acquiescence in a unilateral decision. I suppose that one might say that Mr Kemp told the others of his decision and they accepted it. But that is not to use the word "accept" in the sense of a binding contract being made by an offeree accepting a contractual offer.

Consideration

The fourth element which needs to be present to confirm the presence in law of a binding contract is *"consideration"*. A definition of *consideration* in law is

Something of value given by both parties to a contract that induces them to enter into the agreement to exchange mutual performances.[30]

The question in this case is what consideration Gary Kemp received as a result of the agreement he made to pass half of the publishing income to *Marbelow*. The plaintiff's representative, Mr Sutcliffe, put forward several suggestions to answer this question:

- That it reduced the possibility of dissension within the band due to imbalanced income streams

- That all the band members thought it fair for the publishing income to be shared

- That the band members would perform as members of Spandau Ballet in return (and that without the band performing Gary Kemp's songs there would be less publishing income)

- That they would not leave the band as a result

In examining the first two of these suggestions, Justice Park highlighted the importance of differentiating between *motive* and *consideration*. He accepted that both suggestions provided valid examples of motivation for Gary Kemp to share his publishing income, but did not accept that this amounted to a consideration:

I cannot see how it can have created a contractual consideration for any promise by Mr Kemp. It seems to me to be a clear example of the distinction, drawn in all the text books, between consideration and motive.

He then evaluated the third and fourth suggestion in the light of the legal principle that consideration cannot be something which a party is already obligated to do.

It is sometimes said in abbreviated terms that a promise to perform a pre-existing duty is not good consideration in law.

Clearly, the members of Spandau Ballet were bound by their contracts with *Marbelow* to perform as members of Spandau Ballet, and not to leave the band, so even if it were possible to put forward a convincing case that the third and fourth suggestions did represent something of value which Gary Kemp received in return for the 50% share of publishing income, then it would nevertheless be down to existing obligations and therefore not valid as consideration.

Uncertainty of terms

Finally, the Judge examined the question of *"uncertainty of terms"*. He summarised his main focus as follows:

If a plaintiff invites a Judge to find that conversations in which he has participated created an oral contract it seems to me that - at least in a case where the other party denies that there ever was a contract - the plaintiff's evidence of the conversations needs to satisfy the Judge that there was agreement upon the main contractual terms.

The plaintiffs' problem was that they could provide little evidence to persuade the Judge what had been agreed relating to key terms such as:

- How long the payments of publishing income would continue

- How frequently the payments were to be made

- How the amounts were to be calculated

- What would happen if an individual left the band

Whilst the Judge was happy to accept that there might be, (and had been), occasions when courts had to determine what might have been implied within an agreement when a key term had been omitted, he was not persuaded that he could imply a whole series of terms, when one party maintained that a contract was not in place:

The plaintiffs agree that none of these matters were discussed, and the absence of discussion of them reinforces my conclusion that the contract which they allege was made in the course of discussions was not made at all.

Conclusion

Having dismissed every one of the five key elements he wanted to examine, it is was unsurprising, that Mr Justice Park concluded that, in addition to his decision that the *facts* did not support a case that an oral contract existed between Gary Kemp/*Reformation* and *Marbelow*, there was no case in law either.

One last thing

Having wholly dismissed the Contractual Claim, the Judge examined one last question before moving onto the Copyright Claims:

Did the plaintiffs know about the Termination of Payments from Reformation to Marbelow?

One might ask why he did this, given that it was irrelevant in the light of his decision about the contractual claim. Indeed he recognised that himself:

I could say that the question of whether and when the plaintiffs knew that the payments had been stopped is not important, and therefore I need not deal with it.

The rationale he put forward for considering it regardless was that much time had been devoted to it and that it also influenced the question of whether there was any agreement at all. Certainly, the credibility of the plaintiffs' overall case was potentially damaged further by the weight of evidence against their recollection of events, when discussing whether or not they knew about the payments being stopped. Furthermore, the decision not to accept the plaintiffs' evidence in this area might have some influence on whether the losing parties decided to appeal.

Payments from *Reformation* to *Marbelow* ceased in 1988, but it was not until six years later that Tony Hadley, Steve Norman and John Keeble consulted a solicitor about their rights in relation to the payments. Their explanation for the delay was that they had not been aware that the payments had stopped until 1993. An alternative, and less positive, explanation for the delay is that they *had* known that the payments had stopped in 1988, but were unaware of how important that would be in terms of a reduction in their income. It was only after six years of falling income that they decide to try to assert some rights to the Reformation payments. Mr Justice Park was persuaded by several pieces of evidence that the plaintiffs had been advised that the payments from Reformation were to be stopped, although he did accept that they may not have realised the importance of that at the time:

Steve Dagger explained that personal relationships within the band had broken down at the time so it was inevitable that Gary Kemp would not want personally to tell the other band members of the decision to stop the Reformation payments, and so he asked Dagger to do it. Having done so, Dagger then advised Gary Kemp that they knew. The Judge did not accept that Dagger would have advised Kemp that the deed had been done if he had not done it.

Dagger recalled that he had telephoned each of them to tell them the decision, and had advised them at the same time that Gary Kemp wanted the production credits on the sixth album to read *"Produced by Gary Kemp, Gary Langan and Spandau Ballet."* He remembered them being far more outraged by the second of these pieces of news, perhaps illustrating their lack of awareness of the potential impact of the payments from Reformation stopping.

Dagger recounted two discussions with a tour manager, John Martin, who had worked with the band. In the first he told Mr Martin that he was not looking forward to telling the other band members about the stopping of the payments, and in the second he told Mr Martin of his surprise that their reaction to the news was fairly mild. Martin also confirmed that he believed from his own discussions with the band in 1988 and 1989 that they knew the payments of publishing income had been stopped.

Jackie Vickers recalled Mr Dagger telling her at the time that he had advised the other band members that the payments publishing income had stopped, but that they had been more upset about the album credits.

Miss Vickers also recounted how she would receive phone calls from the band members during the late 1980s and early 1990s, asking about bonuses to be paid to them as they were short of money. Until 1988 they had asked about recording *and* publishing income, but after that they no longer asked about the publishing income.

Gary Langan, the producer of *Heart Like a Sky*, Spandau Ballet's last album, referred to the bitter atmosphere during the recording of the album. He was certain that the withdrawal of the publishing income was one of the explicit complaints which the other band members had made to him about Gary Kemp at the time.

Further evidence was offered regarding conversations between band members and other witnesses which implied *Reformation* would be keeping all publishing income in the future.

The alternative case put by the plaintiffs was that they did not hear anything about the stopping of the payments of the publishing income until 1989, and that they had mistakenly assumed that payments were only being stopped in relation to the final album. They claimed that they had not realised that the decrease in income was down to the loss of publishing income, and that it wasn't until 1993 that they discovered, following a telephone call with Miss Vickers, that publishing income had been stopped on all recordings.

Overall, however, the evidence was strongly in favour of the defendants, and the Judge concluded:

> there is only one finding which I can realistically make: whatever
> the plaintiffs now believe their knowledge to have been in 1988, they
> were told then about the termination of the publishing income
> payments from Reformation to Marbelow.

The copyright claims

Initially, in May 1996, the plaintiffs had only entered a claim on the basis of contract. However two years later they added a copyright claim to that as an alternative claim. The plaintiffs' representative suggested that it would not be pursued if the contractual claim failed. The logic behind this was questioned by the Judge. He felt that it led to the assumption that the plaintiffs were, and would be, willing to allow Gary Kemp to believe he was the copyright holder as long as they received part of the publishing income. It also seemed to imply that they would have put forward a copyright claim in the early 1980s, had Kemp not proposed to pass over 50% of the publishing income. Mr Justice Park's response was blunt:

> *I do not believe it for a moment. All the plaintiffs confirmed in evidence that they had put forward the copyright claim because of legal advice received by them last year, after they had already begun their action. I am of the clear opinion that, until then, it had not crossed their minds that they might have been joint owners of the copyrights.*

There were two main questions to examine:

- Whether the plaintiffs had a valid copyright claim.

- Whether a valid copyright claim would entitle them to claim damages from Reformation/Gary Kemp.

The copyright claim itself related to the musical work only, as it was accepted that Gary Kemp owned the copyright in the lyrics. Furthermore, it only related to works up to and including the fifth album, as there was no claim made in respect of the songs on the band's last album *Heart Like a Sky*.

There were two different arguments put forward to justify the copyright claim. The first argument was that there was "*communal joint ownership*" of the songs, with Gary Kemp's initial ideas being developed jointly into a full composition by the full band. The second argument was that there were individual copyright ownerships due to individual contributions made within specific songs.

Communal joint ownership

It is clear that a definition of "*joint ownership*" is central to the first argument. Section 11(3) of the Copyright Act 1956 (the act in place in 1980s when the songs were written) stated:

> '*work of joint authorship' means a work produced by the collaboration of two or more joint authors in which the contribution of each author is not separate from the contribution of the other author or authors.*

The Judge also referred to section 49 (4) of the 1956 Copyright Act, which defines the point at which a musical work becomes covered in copyright law as being when "*it was first reduced to writing or some other material form.*"

The Judge also cited a range of preceding cases which discussed the concept of joint authorship:

- In *Godfrey v Lees [1995] EMLR 307* Mr Justice Blackburne concluded that "What the claimant to joint authorship of a work must establish is that he has made a significant and original contribution to the creation of the work and that he has done so pursuant to a common design."

- In *Cala Homes (South) Ltd v Alfred McAlpine Homes East Ltd [1995] FSR 818* Mr Justice Laddie accepted that for joint ownership there needed to be collaboration together with a significant contribution from all authors.

- In *Robin Ray v Classic FM PLC [1998] FSR 622* Mr Justice Lightman laid out three characteristics of a joint author as *"a person (1) who collaborates with another author in the production of a work; (2) who (as an author) provides a significant creative input; and (3) whose contribution is not distinct from that of the other author."*

A further case of interest was *Stuart v Barrett* in 1994 where Mr Justice Morison described the process by which *Keep it Dark* produced their compositions:

> *The plaintiff says that he can remember that there was a moment when they stopped playing and the second defendant played a riff on the guitar and looked towards him as though tacitly inviting the plaintiff to put something to support what he was playing. He tried different drum beats and ended up with an off-beat drum pattern which seemed to fit well; and the others joined in, embellishing and changing octave. By the end of the session they had a completed piece of music without words, which became the song 'The Outsider'.[31]*

However Mr Justice Morison was careful to suggest that the conclusions he reached would not always be applicable:

> *Ultimately, as it seems to me, the question of whether a person is a joint author or not within the Copyright Act is simply a question of fact and degree.*

Mr Justice Park summarised the lessons which could be drawn from preceding cases in four elements which needed to be examined when determining whether the members of Spandau Ballet were entitled to joint authorship copyright:

(l) The claimant must have made a contribution of some sort. (2) It must have been significant. (3) It must have been original. (4) It must have been a contribution to the creation of the musical work.

It was therefore necessary to examine the process by which Spandau Ballet's songs were composed. From the evidence given by the band members the process followed the pattern:

- Gary Kemp would compose at home, developing the "the melody, the chords, the rhythm or groove, and the general structure of the song from beginning to end" together with the lyrics.

- He would not write this down, but would present the complete song on acoustic guitar to the other members of the band.

- The rest of the band would learn the song, interpreting it as appropriate according to their roles in the bands.

- The song would then be developed and refined in the recording studio, with the assistance of the record producer and technicians, until the final master was produced.

Mr Sutcliffe, the plaintiffs' representative, tried to make the case that the band's songs were produced through a form of *"jamming"* as described in *Stuart v Barrett*, after Gary Kemp had brought in *"the bare bones of a song."* Interestingly, the plaintiffs had omitted the final album, *Heart Like a Sky*, from their claim, as they argued that it had been developed in a far less collaborative way than the previous albums, due to the breakdown in relationships within the band.

The Judge did not regard their argument as being consistent with the evidence, however, partly because all witnesses agreed that Gary Kemp was very much in charge when it came to the development of the songs, and partly because very few changes were made to songs from the moment they were first presented to the final recording.

A further argument put forward by Mr Sutcliffe was that copyright did not exist in the band's songs until the song was put into material form in the recording studio, and by that stage all members of the band had made their own significant and original musical contributions to the work. The Judge also rejected this argument, on the grounds that the song was already a musical work when presented to the band by Gary Kemp, that the final recorded version did not differ substantially from that initial presentation, and that, whilst the band members played to a high standard, it was not the *"right kind of skill and labour to entitle them to be identified as joint authors."* His decision was supported by opinions from a range of witnesses involved in the process of producing the songs, as well as by comments from an expert musicologist.

As a result of the above, the Judge rejected the argument that the band members were collective joint authors of the songs.

Individual copyright claims

The second basis for the copyright claim was that individual contributions within songs were of a standard which meant that individuals had the right of joint ownership. To evaluate this claim, the Judge had to take each band member in turn.

First he considered the vocalist, Tony Hadley, concluding that whilst he delivered the songs *"in his own memorable style [...] any changes which he made were far too small to make him a joint author."*

Secondly, he examined the case of the drummer, John Keeble. He accepted that Keeble created the drum parts, in terms of determining what beat to strike and when, but again concluded that this contribution consisted of interpretation rather than composition. Keeble himself highlighted the important role played by Kemp in guiding him:

> *If Gary wanted to tell me what he wanted me to play, yes, he would sing roughly a beat to me - you know, he would not show me on the drums - and we began to get a very good working relationship: I knew what was in his head and he knew that I could deliver what was required for the song.*

The Judge did single out one track, however. Entitled *Glow*, the track was issued as an eight minute long, 12 inch single, with a range of drums, played by Mr Keeble, and percussion instruments, played by Mr Norman, having "*substantial and prolonged prominence.*" As a result the Judge concluded that the track was jointly authored by Kemp, Norman and Keeble.

Finally, he considered Steve Norman, who Gary Kemp described as "*the most gifted musician*" of all of them. Norman made contributions on the guitar and saxophone, as well as a range of percussion instruments. He was responsible for one of the most recognisable instrumental contributions on any Spandau Ballet track - the saxophone solo on the track *True* - as well as other improvised fills.

There was much discussion about the nature of the overall range of saxophone fills, which the expert musicologist, Mr Protheroe, described as being "*exactly what was required at that point in the song*" but not "*particularly memorable, tuneful or original.*" He was a little more enthusiastic about the solo in *True*, describing it as "*the only one which he found at all memorable and which he would recognise if played by itself.*" Mr Justice Park also expressed a personal liking for the solo, however then highlighted that it only contributed 35 seconds out of the song's six minutes, or 9% of the song's overall length. (The solo itself starts in the third minute of the song.) Mr Protheroe suggested that it was "*just the sort of thing which any accomplished professional saxophonist would have provided."* Accordingly, he judged that neither such an identifiable contribution, nor any of Mr Norman's other contributions on saxophone, guitar or percussion, were sufficient to allow a successful claim for joint authorship.

Damages

The second question which the Judge had set himself to answer was whether the plaintiffs would have received any damages, had they proved that they were joint authors. Given the Judge's decision on the matter of joint copyright, the question was almost irrelevant, apart from the track *Glow*. Nevertheless the Judge dealt with it, again partly from a point of view of completeness, and partly because he may have wanted to reduce the chance of appeal. If the plaintiffs knew that even if they could persuade an Appeal Court that they were entitled to joint authorship, they would still have to get the Appeal Court to over-rule a decision on whether they were entitled to damages then they would presumably be far less likely to go down that route.

The Judge concluded that the plaintiffs would not have been entitled to any payment. His main rationale for the conclusion was that all agreements and arrangements made by the band and its members throughout the 1980s were implemented on the assumption that copyright in the musical works belonged to Gary Kemp and/or *Reformation*. The band members signed agreements with Chrysalis and CBS which effectively confirmed this. He did not accept Mr Sutcliffe's argument that there was an implied contract between the band members and another party, licensing that other party to exploit their interests in that copyright.

A further rationale which he didn't consider in detail, but suggested he might have used as an alternative justification for concluding that they were not entitled to any payment, related to the principle of estoppel. In effect, Gary Kemp would be able to claim that, relying on the plaintiffs' behaviour in the 1980s, and their responses to his decisions, he had every right to assume that the publishing income belonged to him. He had adapted his lifestyle accordingly, including agreeing *"an onerous divorce settlement."* The Judge observed that it would be

> *unconscionable for the plaintiffs to assert for the first time in 1998 claims to large sums of money which they knew Mr Kemp and Reformation had regarded as belonging to them.*

In summary, the plaintiffs' case failed on every count, except that Steve Norman and John Keeble were granted joint authorship for *Glow*, although they were not entitled to any financial compensation in respect of that ownership.

Following the case, Tony Hadley commented:

> *Let this be a serious lesson to any up and coming artist or band. No matter how good mates you are or whether you were at school together, get a contract.*[32]

On the other hand, Gary Kemp's view was *"I see this as a victory on behalf of all songwriters."*[33]

Analysis

At first sight the claims which Tony Hadley, John Keeble and Steve Norman put forward were not strong ones. There was little evidence to support the argument that the payments from Reformation to Marbelow were contractually binding, and this was reflected in the judgment. Similarly, the argument that they were joint authors who had not got round to asserting their ownership rights appeared to be a shaky one.

There is no doubt that the decision to take the case to court led to substantial costs for the plaintiffs, both in terms of money and in terms of the broken friendship with Gary Kemp. It was estimated that the legal costs they had to pay were around £1m. In an article in The Daily Telegraph in 2011, Tony Hadley commented:

> *Spending 23 days in the High Court in 1999 was a strain and an expensive way to learn about the law. The publishing dispute between Spandau Ballet members concerning royalties was a stressful time, financially. When you lose such a big court case, as I did, you've got to pay out a lot. It cost me hundreds of thousands.*

He lamented the loss of friendship with Gary Kemp, and also blamed the court case for the failure of his first marriage.

It might be asked whether the band were badly advised, and should never have put forward a case which had little chance of success. There were many hurdles which the plaintiffs had to surmount to be successful, and they failed at every one. Following the case, their solicitor, David Wineman, stated that they would be going to the Court of Appeal. This did not happen, however. Perhaps this was because they could not afford to finance it, or perhaps the clarity and comprehensive nature of the Judge's transcript dissuaded them.

Some commentators, however, thought that the judgment regarding joint authorship was flawed. Speaking in 2009 at an Oxford Intellectual Property Seminar[34] Mr Justice Arnold commented "... *the decision is problematic for a number of reasons.*" In particular he suggested that the Judge made no distinction between the original songs presented to the band by Gary Kemp, and the subsequent arrangements recorded by the band. Arnold believed that the distinction was critical, and had the ownership of the arrangement been considered then the outcome might have been different. Of course if one accepts that the final arrangement is different to the original presentation, and has its own separate copyright, then a whole new range of issues are raised. These arose and were examined in detail in the case of *Fisher v Brooker [2009] UKLHL 41* in relation to the song "*Whiter Shade of Pale*".

Furthermore, he questioned the way in which the Judge concluded that there was insufficient creativity and originality in the individual contributions made by soloists to the songs. He raised an interesting question about the 16 bars of solo saxophone in *True*. If Steve Norman was not the composer, then who was? Gary Kemp certainly did not write the notes as they were performed.

There have been examples in similar cases where joint authorship claims have been successful. The 1995 case of *Godfrey v Lees*, referenced above, concerned a dispute between Barclay James Harvest (left) and Robert Godfrey who worked with the band as Musical Director. In court the Judge did accept the claim for joint authorship. However he still did not award royalties as he concluded that the claimant had effectively agreed a royalty-free licence for the defendant to use the work.

When the case of *Fisher v Brooker* went to court (originally in 2006) it could be seen to have similar facts to the Spandau Ballet case. It progressed to the House of Lords in 2009. It concerned the song *Whiter Shade of Pale*, with Mr Fisher, the organist, claiming joint authorship. It was eventually determined that he was a joint author of the *arrangement* which had been recorded some 42 years earlier. Despite the passage of time, it was also concluded that he should be entitled to royalties. However, it was then determined that he had provided a royalty-free licence to other parties for the original recording of the arrangement, and was therefore entitled to no royalties relating to that recording. The only royalties he would receive would be from cover versions and live performances. So even a notionally successful case did not produce much in the way of financial rewards.

Lessons to learn

As a business entity, Spandau Ballet were well structured, and appeared to be well managed. Gary Kemp had set up an arrangement which was more generous than it needed to be. Perhaps if he had not done so then a point of conflict would have emerged earlier, but no-one can say whether such a conflict would have resulted in a resolution by means of implementing a contractual arrangement to pay a share of the publishing income in perpetuity, or the earlier demise of the band. The dispute over royalties was not the catalyst for the band splitting up, however, as it was only when the split up occurred that Gary Kemp chose to change the arrangement.

Many bands avoid the potential for argument over issues relating to joint ownership by declaring that they are joint authors. That would have been a solution in the case of Spandau Ballet, but would it have been fair? Gary Kemp spent time at home working on material for the band, and the other band members were happy to let him do so, recognising that the material he produced was far superior to their material. It is arguable whether Kemp have been willing to give up ownership of his material, even at the exciting early stage of the band when they were all good mates, especially given that he was a self-confessed *"control freak."*

A key point which was certainly illustrated by the case was the importance of publishing income to bands who write their own material, and how it is likely to far exceed recording and live performance income, especially once the band splits up. There have been attempts to change this balance over the past few years, with increased performers' rights, however these are often superseded by contractual arrangements which waive those rights. In similar circumstances now, especially in the light of cases such as *Fisher v Brooker*, it would certainly be sensible for a composer such as Gary Kemp to ensure that an explicit agreement was in place to confirm that his band colleagues did not claim joint authorship rights in the arrangements emanating from his original compositions.

Epilogue

Following the court case, Martin Kemp established a successful acting career, including a regular spot in *Eastenders*. Gary Kemp released a solo album, and also undertook some acting roles, including an appearance in the hit film, *The Bodyguard*. Tony Hadley, Steve Norman and John Keeble had to sell their shares in *Marbelow*, in order to pay off their legal debts. They went on tour together under the name of '*Hadley, Norman and Keeble, ex-Spandau Ballet.*' Tony Hadley enjoyed some success, releasing three albums, being awarded the lead role in the West End production of *Chicago*, and winning the ITV Reality show, *Reborn in the USA*.

In his opening notes, Mr Justice Park commented on the mutual admiration which the band members had for each other:

> *a heartening feature of the evidence was how they remain committed admirers and defenders of each other's artistic qualities. Each of the plaintiffs said in his own way that Gary Kemp was a superb songwriter, and Gary Kemp in his turn was equally complimentary about the musical talents of his former colleagues and present opponents.*

This was perhaps partly why, unlike in some inter-band disputes we have looked at, the band members put aside their legal differences and got back together. Following much speculation in 2009, the band announced in March that year they would do a comeback tour, ironically named the Reformation Tour. The tour was a great success, with tickets for the initial gigs selling out immediately, and further dates being added. They also released a new album, *Once More*, featuring two new songs alongside reworked existing material. They won the Virgin Media Best Comeback Award in 2009. Keeble says now of their court battle:

Win, lose or draw, I don't think anybody comes out of court covered in glory. It wasn't particularly pleasant for anyone. But that's done, and my attitude is: I can't really change that but I can change the bit in front of me.[35]

Keeble was a key figure in getting the band back together. When asked about their initial meeting, Gary Kemp suggested that there were *"some frank exchanges but no apologies."* He went on to say:

Why should anyone apologise? […] We all thought we were right.[36]

In May 16, 2012, Tony Hadley was asked in an interview on *Loose Women* if he would ever tour again with Spandau Ballet. His reply was that it was *"very doubtful"*. Disappointing for fans perhaps, but they should bear in mind that in 2007 he suggested that hell would freeze over before they got back together.

MISREPRESENTATION

THE SPICE GIRLS

The *Spice Girls* were a UK Group, officially established in 1994. They emerged from a group originally known as *Touch*, which was formed by Chris and Bob Herbert, a father and son management team trading as *Heart Management*. The original line-up of *Touch* consisted of Victoria Adams, Melanie Brown, Melanie Chisholm, Geri Halliwell and Michelle Stephenson. However in 1993, Michelle Stephenson left and was replaced by Emma Bunton. Geri Halliwell, the oldest member of the group, apparently came up with the name *"Spice"*. This was later changed to the *Spice Girls*, because the name *"Spice"* was already in use by a rapper in the USA.

In October 1994 the girls left Heart Management, allegedly taking the backing tracks of the songs they had been working on with them. They signed with Simon Fuller from XIX Entertainment in March 1995. Later that year they signed a record deal with Virgin Records and agreed a publishing deal with Windswept Pacific.

The group released their debut single, *Wannabe*, in June 1996, accompanied by a video filmed at St Pancras station in London. The single spent seven weeks at number one in the UK charts. Overall, it was top of the charts in 31 countries, and became the biggest selling single ever by an all-girls group. In July 1996, a feature in Top of the Pops magazine gave the Spice Girls nicknames: Posh (Victoria Adams), Baby (Emma Bunton), Scary (Melanie Brown), Sporty (Melanie Chisholm) and Ginger (Geri Halliwell). These were quickly adopted by the group.

The group's debut album, *Spice*, was released in November 1996. Two million copies were sold in the first two weeks, and it became the biggest selling album of 1996 in the UK, and the biggest selling album of 1997 in the USA. At the same time, Simon Fuller set up a range of valuable sponsorship deals for the group with Pepsi, Walkers, Impulse, Cadbury's and Polaroid. The deal with Pepsi eventually led to the release of a promotional single which fans could get for free, having collected special Pepsi ring-pulls.

In February 1997 the group collected two Brit Awards: one for *Say You'll Be There* as Best Video and one for *Wannabe* as Best Single. The group was not universally popular however. Liam Gallagher, from Oasis, refused to attend the event and commented that, if he did, he would *"probably chin the Spice Girls"*. Later that month, the group out-performed the Beatles, in becoming the first British group to have a US number one with their first single. In March 1997, *Mama/Who Do You Think You Are* went straight into the UK charts at number one, making the *Spice Girls* the first group in history to have four consecutive number one hits. Despite the chart success, the group's first live UK gig did not take place until May 1997, at the Prince's Trust 21st Anniversary Concert. Afterwards Prince Charles admitted to being a fan of the group.

In November 1997, the group members decided to remove Simon Fuller as their manager and do it themselves. That same month, their second album, *Spiceworld*, was released, and went to number one in the album charts. The following month, the *Spiceworld* film was released, eventually grossing £8.5m in the UK, and $30m in the USA. In February 1998, the group embarked on the 102-date *Spiceworld* tour. The following month, their run of number one singles ended, when their seventh single, *Stop*, entered the UK chart at number two. On 31 May 1998 it was officially confirmed, following some days of rumours, that Ginger Spice (Geri Halliwell) had left the Spice Girls, due to *"differences"*. Prince Charles sent the remaining group members a letter of condolence.

The shortened line-up undertook a tour of the US in 1998, and released further successful singles during 1998. They completed the *Spiceworld Tour* at Wembley Stadium. Further singles were released over the next couple of years, and then all was quiet until a reunion in June 2007, under their former manager, Simon Fuller.

Overall, the Spice Girls achieved record sales worldwide of more than 100 million, had nine number one singles, and reported annual earnings of £29.8m in 1998, the highest ever earnings for an all-female group. They agreed a substantial amount of sponsorship and advertising deals, with a wide range of companies and brands, including Aprilia; Cadbury's; Chupa Chups; Walkers Crisps; Pepsi; Polaroid; Impulse; Playstation; Asda; Tesco; Channel Five, Target Stores, and Domino Sugar. They also released a book, and a wide range of merchandise including Spice Girls' dolls.

The sponsorship deal with Aprilia

One of the proposed sponsorship deals which the Spice Girls became involved in was with an Italian manufacturer of motorcycles, called Aprilia. There were four key participants involved in the deal:

- "SGL": a company jointly owned by the Spice Girls, and used to exploit their services.

- "KLP": a company engaged by SGL as their agent in securing sponsorship for their 1998 and 1999 tours.

- "AWS" (Aprilia World Service BV): a company incorporated in the Netherlands, and member of the Aprilia group.

- Aprilia Spa: the company which manufactured the motorcycles which were the subject of the sponsorship.

The sponsorship deal was agreed between SGL and AWS in May 1998, following some months of discussions. The main terms of the agreement were as follows:

- The Spice girls would promote a basic range of air-cooled Sonic scooters, aimed at "fun-loving" teenage girls.

- Aprilia would manufacture and promote a special limited edition scooter named *Spice Sonic*. These would be produced in two special fashion colours: light blue and orange, associated respectively with the public images of Baby Spice (Ms Bunton) and Ginger Spice (Ms Halliwell).

- AWS would pay a sponsorship fee of £400,000 (in three instalments) plus a £112,500 non-returnable royalty advance of £112,500. Royalties would accumulate at £15 per scooter for the first 10,000 scooters sold, and £10 per scooter for subsequent sales. AWS would provide SGL with 20 sonic scooters and 10 Moto Bikes. (Originally the sponsorship fee was to be £450,000 but it was reduced to £400,000 after Aprilia incurred £50,000 costs in a cancelled photoshoots).

- AWS would be publicised as the *"Official Sponsor of SpiceWorld"*, receiving commercial rights for 12 months in Europe, with additional rights in the USA and Japan. The Agreement would last until at least 31 March 1999.

As a result of the agreement, AWS produced promotional material featuring the Spice Girls and the scooters. SGL supplied a logo to be used on the scooters; it consisted of the word *"SPICE"*, with each letter incorporating the likeness of one of the Spice Girls. Importantly the number of group members matched the number of letters in the logo. A promotional video was also produced.[37] Unfortunately, Geri Halliwell left the group before the deal was consummated, and this led to the legal dispute. The full timeline of key events is shown below.

04/03/98	Heads of Agreement signed between SGL & AWS
08/03/98	Sponsorship deal officially announced
09/03/98	Geri Halliwell tells band she has *"had enough"*
Mar 98	Unsuccessful photocalls in Barcelona & Munich
30/03/98	Fax confirms Spice Girls' commitment to agreement
21/04/98	First instalment of £150,000 paid to SGL by AWS
25/04/98	London meeting to discuss Geri Halliwell's future
04/05/98	Second instalment of £150,000 paid to SGL by AWS
04/05/98	Commercial Shoot takes place
06/05/98	Sponsorship Agreement signed
27/05/98	Geri Halliwell leaves
31/05/98	Announcement of Geri Halliwell's departure
01/06/98	Departure of Geri Halliwell confirmed to AWS
06/06/98	AWS letter to SGL confirms that they do not consider Halliwell's departure to be a breach of contract
22/07/98	Writ issued against AWS for non-payment of third instalment/royalty advance (£212,500 + VAT/interest)
26/11/98	AWS submit defence and counterclaim
09/12/98	SGL submit defence to counterclaim
Oct 99	Halliwell's autobiography confirms her departure was discussed in March 98 and agreed on 25/4/98
Feb 00	Trial
24/01/02	Appeal by SGL and AWS

Claim and counterclaim

The claim put forward by SGL was quite simple. They demanded payment of the third instalment of the sponsorship fee, amounting to £100,000 plus the guaranteed royalty amount of £112,500, in line with the contract which was signed on 6th May 1998.

The defence and counterclaim from AWS was far more complex. One section of their claim was in respect of breach of contract. This was perhaps surprising given that they had stated in a letter to SGL on 8th June 1998 that they did not consider the departure of Geri Halliwell to be a breach of contract. This section of the claim was initially for £6.1m, though by the time of the trial it had been reduced to just below £1m. The figure was based on the profits which AWS claimed to have lost due to the fact that the contract had not been fulfilled.

A separate section of their claim was in respect of misrepresentation. They argued that they had entered the agreement with SGL on the assumption that the Spice Girls would continue to have five members. They contended that they had relied on "*an express or implied representation and/or implied term or collateral warranty*" that SGL had no reason to believe that any member might leave the band during the minimum term of their Agreement.

The key elements of AWS's case were as follows:

- At no time during the negotiations between SGL and AWS did SGL mention that there was a possibility that Geri Halliwell might leave the group, even though she had communicated this to the other Spice Girls informally in March 1998, and at a formal meeting which took place in April 1998.

- The marketing materials and logo which were produced to promote the range of Aprilia scooters were approved by SGL, and "*emphasised the distinct and individual image, style and personality of each of the Spice Girls.*" The logo to be used on the scooters consisted of the word "SPICE". Each letter incorporated the likeness of one of the band members.

- Following unsuccessful photoshoots in Barcelona and Munich, a representative of KLP sent a fax on 30 March 1998 to AWS confirming the group's commitment to the sponsorship arrangement. It concluded "*We are confident that over the period of the agreement Aprilia will achieve maximum value and results from the association with the Spice Girls.*"

- Following the fax, AWS arranged a further commercial photoshoot for the 25th and 26th April. This took place successfully, though not until 4th May, after the first instalment had been paid to SGL, and on the day the second instalment was paid, nine days after the meeting to discuss Geri Halliwell's situation had taken place.

Their submission concluded:

> *We consider that the fax of 30th March 1998 contained express representations by SGL as to the commitment of each of the Spice Girls to the future implementation of all the terms of the heads of agreement as subsequently incorporated into the formal agreement to be concluded between SGL and Aprilia. That statement was untrue because SGL knew that the term of the agreement for which provision was made in the heads of agreement was 12 months and that there was a risk that Ms Halliwell would leave after only six of them.*

Overall AWS claimed damages of £434,000, including the return of the £300,000 payments they had made to SGL.

The initial court case

The initial trial took place between 7th February and 14th February 2000 in front of Mrs Justice Arden.[38] She was quick to dismiss the claim in respect of breach of contract, citing the letter which AWS had sent to SGL on 8th June 1998.

In examining the claim for misrepresentation, the Judge considered Section 2 (1) of the Misrepresentation Act 1967:

> *Where a person has entered into a contract after a misrepresentation has been made to him by another party thereto and as a result thereof he has suffered loss, then, if the person making the misrepresentation would be liable to damages in respect thereof had the misrepresentation been made fraudulently, that person shall be so liable notwithstanding that the misrepresentation was not made fraudulently, unless he proves that he had reasonable ground to believe and did believe up to the time the contract was made that the facts represented were true.*

In simple terms, for a party to be liable under the Act there are four elements which need to be satisfied:

- A misrepresentation must have been made

- A contract must have subsequently been made between the parties

- The second party must have suffered a consequential loss

- The first party must, at the time the contract was made, not have believed in, or not had reasonable grounds to believe in, the truth of the facts represented.

The parties did not dispute that a contract had been made, or that AWS had suffered a consequential loss as a result. The key questions to consider therefore were whether SGL had made a misrepresentation to AWS by failing to discuss the possible departure of Geri Halliwell, and whether, at the time the contract was made, they had reasonable grounds to believe that no such departure would occur.

In examining the second of these points, the Judge considered the conversations which had taken place during March and April 1998, when Geri Halliwell announced her intention to leave the group. She accepted that the other four Spice Girls may not have taken Halliwell seriously, but concluded that they, as four Directors and representatives of SGL, were aware that she *might* leave the group in September 1998, within the duration of the Agreement with AWS. As such they did not have reasonable grounds to believe that there was no possibility of such a departure occurring.

The key question which remained therefore was whether or not they had, expressly or impliedly, through their agents or representatives, misrepresented the situation to AWS. A number of elements/incidents were relevant in determining this:

- The signed Agreement which stated that AWS would have *"product endorsement rights of the group of individuals performing under the professional name "Spice Girls" (currently comprising ...)"*

- The fax of 30th March 1998, sent by KLP after Geri Halliwell had initially announced her intention to leave the group. This confirmed the group's commitment to the sponsorship arrangement, and, according to AWS's representative, Ms Fuzzi, motivated her to go ahead with the deal by making payments to SGL and arranging the photo-shoots.

- The logo supplied by SGL for the scooters which consisted of the word *"SPICE"*, with each letter incorporating a picture of one of the Spice Girls. Clearly, this arrangement would not operate effectively in the event that one member of the group left.

- The commercial shoot which took place on May 4th 1998, which all five Spice Girls attended.

Mrs Justice Arden did not accept that there was express misrepresentation within the Agreement which was signed on 6th May 1998. Her view was that the phrase *"currently comprising"* made it clear that there might be a situation in which the make-up of the group changed:

> *Those words were literally true and signal the possibility of future changes in the line-up of the group.*

The fax of 30th March was sent to AWS by KLP (SGL's agents) rather than SGL. Nevertheless, Mrs Justice Arden accepted that the Spice Girls would have been comfortable with its contents. She also accepted that it would have reassured AWS about the proposed agreement, and went so far as to say:

> *given Ms Fuzzi's strong feelings about the Spice Girls lack of commitment I have no doubt that Aprilia would have pulled out at this stage if it had not received this fax.*

However, somewhat puzzlingly, she later concluded that the fax only acted to allay concerns about the photoshoots and that it *"should not in my judgment be construed as having a wide and general effect."* As a result she did not accept it as evidence of misrepresentation.

Mrs Justice Arden *did* believe, however, that the promotional materials depicting the five Spice Girls, and their participation in the photoshoot on 4th May 1998, consisted of

*representation by conduct that SGL did not know, and had no
reasonable ground to believe, that any of the Spice Girls had an
existing declared intention to leave the group before that date [the
end of the Agreement with Aprilia]*

She was clear that the meeting which the group held on the 25th
April 1998 meant that SGL *were* aware that there was a possibility
that one member would leave the group. Their failure to highlight
that possibility to AWS whilst continuing to work with them on
the collaboration consisted of continuing misrepresentation by
conduct. She also believed that this misrepresentation had acted
as an inducement to AWS to confirm the agreement with SGL:

*Given that Aprilia had to sign the agreement to get the right to use
the commercial shoot (and that there was no other reason for it to
sign the agreement except to get the rights thereunder), it seems to
me that the court can infer that indirectly it was induced to enter
the contract by the representations made to it when it made the
shoot.*

Costs and damages

Having decided that SGL was liable for misrepresentation as
described above, a further hearing was held to determine what
payments should be made, and who should be liable for costs.
There were many complicating factors in examining the question
of financial compensation.

The Agreement had been signed between SGL and AWS, but it
was the parent company, Aprilia, who manufactured the scooters,
and distributed them in Italy. As a result, there was confusion
over whether Aprilia's costs and profits should be included in the
calculations.

SGL argued that increases in AWS' profits as distributor of Aprilia
scooters outside Italy should be taken into account when assessing

the benefits it had gained from the aborted association with the Spice Girls. It claimed that such profits would exceed any damages due to AWS. AWS countered this by claiming that there were no additional profits outside Italy as the *Spice Sonic* range flopped, and the sales of basic Sonic scooters had not increased.

There was confusion over figures supplied by AWS which were inconsistent and difficult to interpret. For example, there was dispute over whether or not sales of basic Sonic scooters within Italy had increased, with Mrs Justice Arden having concluded that they had done so, but AWS claiming that they had not.

There was also dispute over whether calculations should incorporate sales and profits on all ranges of scooters. It was clear that the *Spice Sonic* range should be included. However, there was argument over whether the *basic* Sonic range should be included, on the grounds that it was expected that its sales might be affected positively by the association with the Spice Girls. Aprilia also produced a range of liquid-cooled scooters, aimed at young men, who were unlikely to be attracted by the association with the Spice Girls. It was further disputed whether sales increases in the summer of 1998 occurred on account of the association with the Spice Girls, or were simply due to seasonal factors.

It was contested whether a decrease in sales between 1998 and 1999 demonstrated a positive impact from the association with the Spice Girls in 1998, occurred as a knock-on effect on Aprilia's image as a result of the failure of the sponsorship, or was simply a natural decline as the novelty effect of the Sonic Scooters range dissipated.

AWS's claim consisted of five items:

- The *"Fee paid"* of £300,000.

- The *"Value of goods delivered"* amounting to £39,699 in respect of the value of 19 scooters and 8 Aprilia *"Moto"* bikes delivered (to SGL) under the terms of the contract.

- *"The scooters"* This was a credit against any sums owed by SGL to AWS, in respect of profits earned on Spice Sonic scooters which had been sold.

- *"Advertising and promotional material"* This represented costs paid by Aprilia (not AWS) in respect of a marketing campaign associated with the Spice Girls.

- Costs for the *"cancelled New York photo call"*

In the event, Mrs Justice Arden communicated her decisions through three judgments. The third judgment reversed one of the conclusions in the second judgment, in relation to the inclusion of Aprilia's costs and profits. Her final judgment, published on 13th June 2000, stated that

- SGL should pay AWS £39,699 (plus VAT) in respect of the value of scooters they received as part of the Agreement.

- No credit was due to SGL from AWS for any additional benefits received by AWS (or Aprilia) as a result of the sponsorship agreement.

- The remaining sums of £100,000 and £112,500 would, if paid, be recoverable back by AWS on account of SGL's infringement of Section 2(1) of the Misrepresentation Act 1967, and therefore no payments either way should be made.

Mrs Justice Arden also made an order relating to costs, requiring AWS to pay SGL's costs relating to what she considered to be an unjustified claim for breach of contract and express misrepresentation. She required SGL to pay 75% of AWS's other costs up until 13th December 1999, and 60% of their costs after that date.

The final position following the trial therefore was that SGL had received £260,301 (net) plus 19 scooters and 8 Moto Bikes from AWS for the aborted sponsorship agreement. However, they were responsible for paying substantial legal costs incurred by themselves and AWS.

Following the hearing, Melanie Chisholm, repeated the Spice Girls' claim that they did not know Geri Halliwell was leaving. She told BBC Radio 1's Newsbeat:

> We were in the right. If we have lost the case then justice has not been done. We did not know Geri was going to leave. But hey-ho, life goes on.

The appeal

Following the initial trial, both parties decided to appeal.

AWS appealed against the narrow interpretation of misrepresentation which the judge had taken, claiming that she should have accepted their wider view that SGL had been guilty of misrepresentation throughout the negotiations. They claimed that there was a series of representations by SGL which were either false when made, or which should have been corrected once SGL were aware that they were false, and that these induced AWS into the Agreement and caused losses for AWS.

AWS also appealed against the decision that they should pay 10% of all costs, on the grounds that Mrs Justice Arden had no good reason for ordering a successful party to pay for the costs.

SGL claimed that the judge was wrong that there was misrepresentation by conduct. They further contended that, even if there was misrepresentation it was only that SGL had no grounds to believe that any of the Spice Girls would leave before September 1998. They also claimed that AWS did not understand the representation in the sense alleged and was not induced by any alleged misrepresentation to enter into the Agreement.

SGL appealed against the decision that no credit should be allowed for benefits obtained by AWS from the Agreement. They argued that AWS had failed to prove that they had made a real loss as a result of the Agreement.

As a consequence of the above, SGS appealed against the decision that none of the additional contractual payments should be made to them by AWS.

The Appeal Hearing took place on 24th January 2002, before the Vice Chancellor Sir Andrew Morritt, Lord Justice Chadwick, and Lord Justice Rix[39]. The Appeal Judges accepted AWS's first grounds for appeal. Unlike Mrs Justice Arden, they regarded SGL's actions in setting up the photoshoot and agreeing the promotional materials as part of an on-going and continual process which implied that, in SGL's knowledge, there was no possibility of a member of the Spice Girls leaving before the Agreement with AWS was complete.

This is not a case of an isolated representation made at an early stage of on-going negotiations. It is the case of a series of continuing representations made throughout two months' negotiations leading to the Agreement. Later representations gave added force to the earlier ones; earlier representations gave focus to the later ones. It is in this context, not the much more limited one the Judge adopted, that the submissions for SGL as to inducement and reliance must be considered.

They also interpreted the phrase *"currently comprising"*, which was contained in the Agreement, in a different manner to Mrs Justice Arden, who had felt it simply implied that there might be a different set-up in the future.

The Appeal Judges observed:

> *to say that the Spice Girls currently comprised the five named individuals without going on to say that one of them was going to leave within the period of the Agreement was false when made. What was omitted rendered that which was actually stated false or misleading in the context in which it was made.*

The Appeal Judges also placed a broader view of the fax of the 30th March. Rather than simply seeing it as a confirmation of the group's commitment to the photocell, they saw it as being *"express representations by SGL as to the commitment of each of the Spice Girls to the future implementation of all the terms of the heads of agreement."*

They further stated that even if SGL had not *initially* believed that one of the group members might leave, they had a responsibility to advise AWS of this possibility as soon as they were aware of it. To support this they cited Lord Justice Romer in *With v O'Flanagan [1936]:*

> *If A with a view to inducing B to enter into a contract makes a representation as to a material fact, then if at a later date and before the contract is actually entered into, owing to a change of circumstances, the representation then made would to the knowledge of A be untrue and B subsequently enters into the contract in ignorance of that change of circumstances and relying upon that representation, A cannot hold B to the bargain.*[40]

Their view was that rather than correct any early misinterpretations about the stability of the group as a five piece, SGL continued in the same manner in their statements and conduct. They therefore concluded that the misrepresentation that took place was on-going and cumulative, rather than restricted to two individual events. They also confirmed that it would still have been misrepresentation even if the parties had not believed in the seriousness of Halliwell's threat to leave the group. However they were clear that, in any event, the meeting of 25th April should have dispelled any doubt about the seriousness of Halliwell's intentions.

The Appeal Judges then considered the question of whether the misrepresentations had acted as an inducement to AWS to sign the Agreement. Whilst they accepted that no witnesses had been called to provide evidence of such inducement, they agreed with Mrs Justice Arden that had AWS known about Halliwell's possible departure, they would not have signed the Agreement as it stood:

It is inconceivable [...] that AWS would have entered into those commitments had it been told of Ms Halliwell's declared intention to leave in September 1998. It might have entered into some other agreement with a view to cutting its losses but that was not alleged by SGL.

Having determined that SGL *was* guilty of misinterpretation in a wider sense, the question which then needed to be re-examined was how much damages, if any, AWS were due, and whether AWS would have to pay some or any of the remaining contractual amounts to SGL. In the original trial, Mrs Justice Arden had concluded that AWS should have to pay damages of £39,699, being the cost of the scooters supplied, and that no further payments were due in either direction.

After much consideration the Appeal Judges concluded that there was insufficient evidence to support the claim that AWS should provide SGL with credit for increased profits as result of the association, and that obtaining further evidence would not be worth the effort, especially as both parties had requested that the court make its decision based on the evidence available:

It is worth bearing in mind just how refined would be the assessment which would have to be made if it were relevant and necessary to calculate the credit which AWS might have to give in respect of enhanced sales of standard Sonic scooters outside Italy. [...] The possibilities that any enhanced sales might be due either to seasonal factors or to novelty [...] would have to be considered. The question of whether any credit due to profits on enhanced sales would have to be set off first against the £300,000 payments prior to the Agreement would have to be determined. The question of whether AWS had earned any profit by distributing the scooters would have to be examined. There is no evidence about that at all.

Finally, the Appeal Judges considered the question of whether Mrs Justice Arden was correct in ordering AWS to pay 10% of SGL's costs for two of the issues which were originally pursued. Contrary to Mrs Justice Arden, they felt that it had been reasonable for AWS to pursue the claims to trial and therefore concluded *"that the Judge's findings that AWS acted unreasonably in pursuing the two issues which she identified cannot be supported."* Accordingly the requirement for them to pay 10% of the costs was withdrawn.

The final result then was that SGL had still received £260,301 (net) plus 19 scooters and 8 Moto Bikes from AWS for the aborted sponsorship agreement. However, they were now responsible for paying substantial legal costs incurred by themselves and AWS at both the initial trial, *and* the Appeal.

It is difficult to be certain how much this amounted to. The Daily Telegraph's report on 24th Jan 2002 estimated that it would cost about £1million in legal costs, although SGL's representatives claimed it would be nearer £500,000. Although it was widely reported after both court cases that the Spice Girls would be paying damages of £400,000 plus, in the event they did not have to do so.

Analysis

Many commentators looking at the facts of the *Spice Girls v Aprilia* case seem somewhat surprised to discover that it was the Spice Girls suing Aprilia, rather than vice versa. Looked at objectively, they had entered an agreement (as a group of five), failed to deliver, and had already received £300,000 for their efforts. Interestingly, a spokesman for Aprilia was quoted in the Guardian after the initial judgment in February 2000, commenting on how astonished they were to receive a writ from SGL in October 1999:

> *Aprilia would not have sued if the Spice Girls had not brought their claim, and were deeply disappointed when they did.*

It seems that Aprilia were willing to write off their losses, but SGL were not. The Agreement with AWS was signed a few months after they had fired their manager, Simon Fuller. The transcript of the Appeal comments that:

> *At that time the Spice Girls had no manager. Some of the functions of a manager were undertaken by Mr Andrew Thompson ("Mr Thompson") a solicitor and partner in Lee & Thompson.*

It is possible that their approach might have been different if a manager had been involved in the negotiations. Would a manager have advised them to be more open about the possibility of one of the group members leaving, to avoid future liabilities? Would a manager have suggested that, having received £300,000 for the Agreement, they should "let sleeping dogs lie" rather than stirring things up by taking legal action to recover the remaining £212,500. Once they had started down that road there was always a chance they would lose and that it would cost them substantial sums in legal costs. To an impartial observer, their case was not a strong one, and it was exceedingly unlikely that Aprilia/AWS would simply roll over and pay them the £212,500. In the event one might consider that they were fortunate not to have to repay some of the £300,000 they had received.

In the initial court case, the group members seemed relatively unaware of the nature of the Agreement with AWS. Geri Halliwell put this down to having other concerns: *"When you're an artist, you're an artist"*(!) None of them appeared at the Appeal Case. One has to question where the decision to take action against AWS came from. Maybe they were badly advised, but one doesn't really need hindsight to conclude that it was not a wise one, and probably not a path that Simon Fuller would have taken.

So what lessons can be learned? The *Spice Girls v Aprilia* case is cited as a key case in establishing precedent for misrepresentation by conduct in English Law. If you are aware of a possible issue which the other party should be aware of, but your conduct attempts to conceal that from the other party, then you may be found guilty of misrepresentation by conduct. It is a risk which you may choose to take in contract negotiations, but, as the Spice Girls found, it may come back and bite you at a later stage.

Perhaps a more obvious lesson is to know when to leave things alone, and when to recognise that you may actually have done quite well out of a situation. Had the Spice Girls stepped away from legal action, they would have saved themselves between £500,000 and £1,000,000 in legal costs. Who knows, that might have reduced their need to reform in 2007 (ironically under the manager they fired) and the world might be a better place.

COPYRIGHT, PLAGIARISM & SUMMARY JUDGMENTS

WHO WANTS TO BE A MILLIONAIRE?

Celador Productions Limited was formed in 1983 as an independent production company. It was responsible for devising and producing the TV quiz show, *Who Wants to Be a Millionaire?* *(WWBM)*. It also co-produced *Slumdog Millionaire*, a film centred on a character who is competing in the Indian version of the programme. In 2006 Celador sold the rights for *WWBM*, and all UK episodes, to a Dutch Company called 2waytraffic, for £106m. In 2008, 2waytraffic was sold to Sony Pictures Television for £137.5m.

The first episode of *WWBM* was broadcast on ITV on 4 September 1998. By 2012 over 580 episodes had been broadcast in 29 series. At its peak in 1999, it was watched by 19 million viewers. Its format was also successfully exported across the world. In 1995 a survey by the Format Recognition and Protection Association (FRAPA) reported that the *WWBM* format had been sold to 106 countries. Protecting TV formats is known to be difficult, as they are not directly protected by copyright legislation. The strategy used for successfully generating income from the *WWBM* format was analysed in a 2011 report on exploiting TV Formats, produced by FRAPA and Bournemouth University.[41] At times, the strategy has led Celador into court proceedings. For example, in 2000, they successfully acted against Danmarks Radio and Television to prevent them broadcasting a show called *Double or Quits*, which was allegedly based on *WWBM*.

They were less successful in 2004, in *Arief International v Celador*. Celador had terminated a perpetual license granted to Arief, after they had subcontracted production of the show to another party. They awarded a new contract to an Australian company. Arief took action in a UK court and won the case, with Celador ordered to pay £1m in damages plus legal costs, estimated to amount to a similar sum.

Celador's biggest success in a court case took place in July 2010 against the Disney Corporation, following a legal battle which lasted eight years. They were awarded £177m in damages after the Disney Corporation allegedly used creative accounting to hide profits which should have been due to Celador from a profit-sharing arrangement set up when the programme was shown in the USA.

Probably the most famous court case Celador was involved in took place in 2003, after a contestant, Major Charles Ingram, won the £1m prize, but was subsequently accused of having cheated, by collaborating with his wife and another contestant. After a trial at Crown Court, Ingram and his wife Diana were given 18-month suspended prison sentences and fined £15,000. The other contestant, Tecwen Whittock, was given a 12-month suspended sentence and fined £10,000. The case cost the Ingrams £115,000 included legal costs, and of course they did not get the £1m prize money. The case was the subject of a documentary called Major Fraud, which can be viewed (in eight parts), on YouTube.

This chapter focuses on cases relating to the origin of *WWBM*. A number of individuals have brought cases claiming that the programme was copied from their idea. For example, in 2003 John J Leonard from Sydney, Australia, claimed that he had previously devised a format resembling *WWBM*. He was unable to finance legal action against Celador in the UK, however he did publish a book entitled *Millionaire*; it recounted the story of how he claimed to have created the show.

Celador received three further challenges of a similar nature in 2003. It applied for *summary judgment* against all three actions, and the hearings were held in one session on 21 October 2004, before the Vice Chancellor, Sir Andrew Morritt.

What is meant by Summary Judgment?

Summary Judgment is a fast-track process which either party (or the judge) can use in a civil case to settle the case without a trial, when there is no dispute over the material facts of the case. Parties may provide evidence and submissions to support their request for summary judgment. A court may listen to verbal submissions, or may make a decision based solely on supporting evidence. A court may grant full or partial judgment; for example it may accept a claim, but place the burden for determining damages on a subsequent hearing. Alternatively, a court may strike out part of a claim.

Rule 24.2 of the Ministry of Justice rules states that summary judgment may be granted by a court against a claimant or defendant, on the whole of a claim or on a particular issue, if it considers there is no real prospect of the claimant or defendant succeeding, and if there is no other compelling reason why the case or issue should be dealt with at a trial.

The three claims against Celador and ITV

There were three claims for summary judgment considered by the Vice Chancellor, Sir Andrew Morritt on 21st October 2004:[42]

- Celador Productions Limited and Melville

- Boone and ITV Network and Another (Celador)

- Baccini and Celador Productions Limited

The first task undertaken by the court was to examine Celador's account of how *WWBM* was devised and developed. Their account of this process is outlined below.

An initial programme idea was developed by David Briggs in 1995. Briggs had worked with Chris Tarrant at Capital Radio, and had an impressive track record of working in TV and Radio, particularly with competitions and quizzes. The programme would be called *Cash Mountain*, and features of the original idea included:

- Multiple choice questions, the value of which doubled at each stage

- Contestants being given an option to leave with their winnings after answering a question successfully

- Contestants losing their accumulated winnings if they answered a question incorrectly

- Prize money to be funded by premium line calls from potential contestants

- Chris Tarrant as presenter

A written proposal for the idea was sent to Michael Whitehill and Steven Knight, who Briggs had worked with previously, and who worked as freelance writers and creators for Celador Productions in October 1995. The proposal included further developments:

- Contestants to be selected by answering six questions correctly on a premium number telephone line

- A process by which several contestants would compete together answering multiple choice questions, until a point at which only the leading contestant would continue to try to win the prize money.

- A series of twenty questions, starting at £10 and ending up at £52,428,800

The idea was developed further between October 1995 and February 1996, in discussion with Paul Smith, the Chief Executive of Celador Productions who was supportive of the project. In February 1996 an eight page written proposal for *Cash Mountain Version 2* was published, bearing a cover sheet which stated "© *Celador Productions 1996*". The proposal now contained more features which will be familiar to those who have watched *Who wants to be a Millionaire*:

- 21 questions leading to a £1 million pound top prize

- A "safe haven" once contestants had answered a certain number of questions

- Three "*helping hands*" available to contestants if they got stuck - "*ask the audience*"; "*phone a friend*" and "*50/50*"

The proposal was pitched to Senior Executives at ITV during the latter part of February 1996, and as a result, qualitative market research was commissioned. This proved positive, although it did suggest that a new name was needed, and that the word "*million*" needed to be emphasised in the title. Despite the positive feedback, Paul Smith received a letter from Ms Claudia Rosencrantz, Controller of Network Entertainment at ITV, advising him that they would not be commissioning the programme. Following this, Smith offered the programme to Channel 5, Channel 4, Sky, London Weekend Television and Carlton, and whilst they all showed initial interest, none agreed to commission the programme.

Further attempts to persuade ITV to reconsider were unsuccessful, however in September 1997 a new Director of Programmes, David Liddiment, was appointed at ITV. A revised proposal, (*Cash*

Mountain Version 3), was submitted to him, incorporating some of the suggestions which came from the qualitative market research. Following further discussions, and a fourth version being produced, agreement was reached in April 1998 to commission the programme under the revised title: *Who wants to be a Millionaire?* The number of questions had also been reduced to fifteen. Further minor amendments were made to the format, following a pilot programme in August 1998, and the first programme was then broadcast in September 1998.

A detailed account of the development of the programme, and a colourful description of Liddiment's meeting with Paul Smith was published in 1999 in the Independent Newspaper.[43]

Celador Productions Limited and Melville

Mr Alan Melville's claim was submitted in a 35 page written statement, supported by appendices. Melville claimed to have sent an initial proposal for a show called *Millionaire's Row - Bingo* to a number of TV companies in early 1995. He created a revised version of the same proposal, called *Millionaire's Row - Slot Machine* and posted it to himself, in order to provide evidence of its existence, on 20th May 1995. He declared that the following exchanges of correspondence had taken place with Carlton TV:

- Copy of the initial proposal sent to them on 14th August 1995

- Letter sent to them with a revised proposal, two or three weeks later

- Receipt dated 29th August 1995 received from Carlton

- Rejection letter dated 25th September 1995 received from Carlton

- Telephone call made by Melville to Carlton requesting the return of the proposal

- Photocopy letter, dated 20th October 1995, received by Mr Melville, together with the initial proposal

- Telephone call made by Melville to Carlton requesting the return of the *revised* proposal. During the call, he was advised that they had only ever received the *initial* proposal

Following this rejection, Melville sent copies of his proposals to two other companies, (Granada and Action Time), and received rejection letters from both companies. In 1998, whilst living in Tenerife, he read a newspaper report about *WWBM*. On returning to the UK he watched the first programme. Believing that it was very similar to his revised proposal, and noting that Carlton was included in the credits, he reached the conclusion that Carlton had passed his proposal on to Celador, who had incorporated features of his proposal in their development of *Cash Mountain Version 1* to *WWBM*. He specifically noted that 4 from 23 relevant features in his revised proposal were included in *Cash Mountain Version 1*; 9 of them were included in *Cash Mountain Version 2*; and 22 of them were included in the first episode of *WWBM* broadcast in September 1998.

Melville provided no specific evidence that any of those involved in the development of *WWBM* had seen his revised proposal, simply relying on the similarities he had pointed out, and on the existence of interaction and collaboration between Celador and many of the TV companies he had sent the proposal to.

Celador's response

Celador countered by suggesting that Melville had no real evidence to prove that his revised proposal was even in existence prior to the submission of his initial complaint to them in May

1999. They further suggested that even if he could prove that the revised proposal had existed prior to then, he could not provide satisfactory evidence that it had been sent to *any* TV company, or that the individuals involved in the development of *WWBM* had seen it. They observed that there was confusion in the correspondence which supported those suggestions. Their representative concluded by stating that Mr Melville's case was *"riddled with contradictions, implausibilities and unsupportable assertions as to be plainly incredible"* and went so far as to say that the evidence Melville had presented to prove that the revised proposal had existed in May 1995 was a *"concoction"*.

The Vice Chancellor concluded that the central issue to be determined was whether or not the revised proposal existed in 1995. If it had not existed, then it could not have been sent to the TV companies, and could not have been copied by those who developed *WWBM*. Conversely, if it *had* existed, then, in his view, it would be natural to assume that it *would* have been sent to the companies, and *would* have been seen by the relevant individuals. He concluded that the evidence was not clear enough for him to grant summary judgment on such an issue, as much would depend upon the credibility of Mr Melville under cross-examination, and upon any additional evidence, which might be produced. As he observed:

> *to take a hypothetical example, the discovery of a letter dated November 1995 in the files of a TV company acknowledging receipt of the Revised Proposal would cast a new light on some of the more curious features of Mr Melville's case.*

He therefore dismissed Celador's claim for summary judgment to allow a trial to examine the possibilities and evidence in more depth.

Boone and ITV Network and Another (Celador)

Mr Timothy Boone's claim against ITV and Celador was submitted to the court on 14th October 2003, alleging "*infringement of copyright and misuse of confidential information.*"

The substance of Mr Boone's claim was that in October 1997 he had submitted a proposal for a show called *HELP!* to a company called Talent TV. Talent TV subsequently submitted the format to Claudia Rosencrantz, the Controller of Network Entertainment at ITV. The *HELP!* format was developed by Boone in association with a Mr Bull, who maintained an interest in the copyright ownership. Boone claimed that their rights had been infringed by the production and broadcasting of *Who wants to be a Millionaire*.

Celador and ITV submitted that Boone's claim should be dismissed, first because it was an abuse of the court process, and secondly, because of insufficient evidence.

Abuse of court process

The claim that Boone's case was an abuse of court process related to a previous case taken out against ITV two years earlier. The case was instituted by a company called Watch TV who claimed, on behalf of Mr Bull, (Boone's former partner), that *WWBM* infringed copyright in a quiz game called *HELP!* Mr Bull had assigned his interest in *HELP!* to Watch TV. He had also fallen out with Boone, over the strategy to employ to try to obtain compensation from ITV and, as a result, Boone found himself to be a defendant in the earlier case, alongside ITV. However, on 5th August 2002 Boone reached an agreement with Watch TV for the proceedings against him to be withdrawn. At the same time, ITV successfully obtained summary judgment to dismiss the claim against them on the grounds that there was insufficient evidence. Watch TV obtained permission to appeal against this, however the company was subsequently struck off the register of companies, and on 9th October 2003 a court ruled that no further action could be taken in the case.

Mr Boone's case was instituted five days later on 14th October 2003. It was supported by an eleven page document which was substantially the same as a fourteen page document submitted by Watch TV in support of their case. Celador and ITV maintained that submitting the case after the Watch TV case had been dismissed, using supporting material which was substantially the same, was an abuse of process. They suggested that Boone could have issued an additional claim of his own, (known as a "*Part 20*" claim), against Celador and ITV whilst the Watch TV case was in progress.

The Vice Chancellor agreed with Celador and ITV's submission:

> *In my view Celador and ITV have established that Mr Boone should have pursued his claim by Part 20 proceedings in the Watch TV action and the institution and prosecution of these proceedings is an abuse of the process as claimed. At the time of the Watch TV action Mr Boone was represented by Solicitors. The claim then made by Watch TV was the same as that now made by Mr Boone. It was artificial to treat the Watch TV claim as made only in relation to the half the beneficial interest in the copyright vested in Watch TV (sic) leaving Mr Boone free to bring such proceedings in relation to the other half as he thought fit. The grounds on which Mr Boone now relies, namely alleged falsification of documents, is the same as the ground on which he relied in June 2002.*

Having determined that, in his view, Boone's claim was an abuse of process, the Vice Chancellor nevertheless went on to examine whether or not he would have had a chance of success in his claim, had it gone ahead.

The case itself

Celador and ITV maintained that by the time Ms Rosencrantz saw the pitch regarding *HELP!*, they had already completed *Cash Mountain Version 3*. Accordingly, it would not have been possible for features which were included in that version to have been copied from *HELP!* Furthermore, they stated that there was no evidence that Celador had seen any version of *HELP!* and therefore any knowledge they had of it could only have come as a result of the pitch made to Ms Rosencrantz. They maintained that the pitch would have been drawn from a short 2-4 page summary of the proposal, rather than the eleven page document submitted as part of Boone's claim. Finally, they observed that infringement would only have taken place if a substantial part, rather than just individual elements, of the work had been copied. The case cited in support of this final point was *Norowzian v Arts (No. 2) [2000]* - the Guinness advert case.

Boone put forward a complex account of how he believed documents had been altered by Celador and ITV in order to support their case. He employed a forensic document examiner who agreed that some parts of key reports had been produced at different times, but emphasised that "*it is not possible to interpret the significance of this.*" The Vice Chancellor undertook his own examination, and reached the conclusion that it would not be possible for Boone to satisfy any court that documentation had been falsified or modified in the manner he had claimed. As a result he concluded that

> *the development of Cash Mountain had reached the stage indicated in Cash Mountain Version 3 before any version of HELP! was communicated by Mr Kaye Cooper to Ms Rosencrantz on or about 30th October 1997. Accordingly if any elements of the latter are to be found in the former it cannot be the result of copying.*

He then continued by examining whether elements added to the programme after *Cash Mountain Version 3* could possibly have been copied from *HELP!* In doing so, he did accept that the full eleven page summary could be used as evidence. However, of seven elements which he identified as having been added after *Cash Mountain Version 3*, two showed no similarity at all, and four were described by the Vice Chancellor as being no more than *"the application of well-known presentational techniques."* In his analysis, he accepted the comparison with the lack of copyright subsisting in the techniques used in the film in the Guinness advertisement.

The claim regarding the remaining element perhaps illustrated the weakness of the case. It related to the titles of the two programmes: *"Who wants to be a Millionaire?"* and *"HELP!"* Boone claimed that there was a similarity in that both titles were also titles of popular songs. The Vice Chancellor described this suggestion as *"manifestly absurd."* In conclusion, he confirmed that he would provide summary judgment as requested by Celador and ITV as he saw no need for the evidence to be examined at a trial.

Baccini and Celador Productions Limited

Mr John Baccini's claim began in December 2003. He took action against Celador and ITV, and against Paul Smith, David Briggs, Steven Knight, Michael Whitehill and Claudia Rosencrantz, claiming infringement of copyright and misuse of confidential information, in relation to a board game called *Millionaire*, and a game concept called *BT Lottery*.

In his summary of Baccini's case, the Vice Chancellor observed that *"It is not easy to determine exactly what his claim is."* However he summarised the facts of the case as follows:

- Mr Baccini created a board game known as *Millionaire* in 1982, and an outline for a game called BT Lottery, in 1990.

- He sent *Millionaire* to Complete Communications Corporation Ltd ("CCC"), the holding company of Celador, in 1995, though there was some uncertainty over exactly what he sent to them.

- He sent *Millionaire* to ITV and CCC in January 1996. Within his claim he provided copies of what he claimed to have sent, including three pages describing the TV format.

- On reading about *WWBM* in 1999, he recognised within it features of the *Millionaire* board game, and the fundraising aspects incorporated within BT lottery.

Baccini supplied details of the similarities he believed existed between his games and *WWBM*:

- the £1m prize

- the Title of Millionaire

- multi-choice questions

- the Safe Zones at £1,000 and £32,000

- the fastest foot concept

- the premium phone line

- the Prize Fund

- the pool of contestants

- the Mechanics

There was a substantial delay between Baccini becoming aware of *WWBM* in 1999, and the submission of his claim to the court in 2003. The explanation for this delay was that he had spent a year in prison from mid-1998, that some of his belongings had been taken away when he was arrested, and that it was not until late 2002 that he discovered some relevant documentation in his son's house.

Celador's response to the claim was a denial that they had ever seen any of the documents Baccini had claimed to have sent to CCC or ITV. They maintained that there was no credible evidence that the documents had been sent, and that the alleged similarities were not sufficient to allow the court to infer copying.

Given the dispute over whether the documents had been seen by the defendants or not, the Vice Chancellor made it clear that the key issue to consider in deciding whether or not to grant summary judgment related to the level of similarity between Baccini's games, and the programme itself. His first conclusion was that there was no real similarity with the board game. However, he *did* believe that there were sufficient similarities between the format for the TV game and the programme:

> *In my view the extent of the similarities between the TV format for Millionaire and WWM (sic) as transmitted are capable of giving rise to an inference of copying a substantial part. Similarly they are capable of being corroborative of Mr Baccini's assertion that he sent the documents to CCC and ITV in March 1995 or January 1996.*

Whilst he accepted that there were some difficult questions relating to Baccini's case, he concluded that Baccini had the right for his *"credibility and honesty"* to be evaluated in a full trial and accordingly dismissed the application for summary judgment.

Outcomes and analysis

It is important to remember that in these cases, the defendants were simply asking for summary judgment, so the decision was not the final outcome. Following the decisions, Celador appeared to be determined to fight the cases in court. A spokesperson commented:

> We are staggered that these cases have gone this far and we contest their claims in the strongest possible terms. Who Wants To Be A Millionaire is a wholly original idea created by Celador, and we will rigorously defend that position. [44]

However, neither case progressed to a full court case, and Celador later confirmed in a statement in 2005 that out-of-court settlements had been agreed with Melville and Baccini. These settlements included confidentiality clauses so we have no idea of their size.

It is difficult to know why Celador would have reached such agreements. It might be that there was compelling evidence against them in both cases. On the other hand, they may have concluded that such a settlement would be cheaper and less risky than taking on two individuals in court, who might not have the resources to pay Celador's costs in the event that Celador won. Furthermore, the Vice Chancellor had stated that he believed that Melville and Baccini had "real prospects of success" in their cases. Celador might have found this compelling motivation to settle the cases before reaching court.

The cases highlight the issues facing production companies when developing new programmes. It is worth noting that many film production companies have a policy of returning unsolicited scripts to their sender, marked as "unopened and unexamined" to avoid possible accusations of copying. It also highlighted the issues facing individuals who pitch their creative ideas to potential partners. The Vice Chancellor referred to Mr Boone's conviction that production companies are fundamentally dishonest, and that he was a victim of this dishonesty:

He believes that they receive from free-lance writers, such as himself, a very large number of original ideas for TV programmes from which they feel free to select one or more elements for incorporation into their own. He complains that the person who had the idea receives neither acknowledgement nor compensation.

In support of that contention Mr Boone referred to an extract from *The Television Programme Proposals Code of Practice*[45], which seemed to encourage the process of using creative material submitted to production companies, without being clear on how those who submitted the material should be rewarded:

similar, if not identical, creative material may be submitted to a receiver by different originators at different times. This code does not restrict the freedom of receivers to select the best creative material from the best talent in accordance with commissioning and scheduling priorities.

The extract was, perhaps unsurprisingly, chosen carefully, and did not reflect the whole context of the code, which tries to provide guidance on dealing with submitted material in a manner which is fair both to the originator and the receiver. The code can be viewed on BECTU's website, and it is certainly true to say that none of the parties in the above cases followed it very closely, though it is impossible to determine how the different the outcomes would have been had they done so.

TRADEMARKS

APPLE CORPS VS APPLE COMPUTERS

Apple Music Limited was formally established in December 1967, changing its name, in a play on words dreamed up by Paul McCartney, to Apple Corps in February 1968. The Company was set up because the Beatles had been advised that they needed a business venture in order to shelter £2m of their income from the taxman.

The name Apple apparently came from Paul McCartney, on the grounds that *"A is for Apple"* is the first thing which children are taught when they learn to read. McCartney was also responsible for the choice of logo, inspired by a painting by Belgian surrealist artist, René Magritte. The painting, called *Le Jeu du Morre*, was purchased for Paul McCartney by his friend, the London art dealer, Robert Fraser. It featured an apple with words *"Au revoir"* written across it. The full story of how the painting inspired Paul McCartney can be read in Andrew Graham-Dixon's archive.[46] The Company adopted a full green apple for their logo, and used an apple cut in half for the B-side of records.

Apple Corps Limited bought 80% of the shares in the original Beatles company, and all income generated by the Beatles' activities, apart from songwriting royalties, was channelled through the company. The company was owned equally by all four Beatles; it is still owned by the surviving two Beatles, and by John Lennon and George Harrison's estates.

The Beatles' manager, Brian Epstein, was central to the establishment of Apple, but died suddenly in August 1967. Nevertheless, the Beatles continued with the plans, originally trying to work with Epstein's brother Clive, before setting up the venture on their own as he did not want to work with them. In February 1968, the Company registered the Apple trademark in forty-seven countries, and registered a range of companies, including Apple Electronics; Apple Films; Apple Management; Apple Music Publishing; Apple Records and Apple Retail.

In addition to managing the Beatles' income, the aim of Apple Corps was to support artists who needed money for worthwhile artistic projects. In a press conference in New York in 1968, McCartney explained their vision:

> *We really want to help people, but without doing it like a charity or*
> *seeming like ordinary patrons of the arts. We're in the happy*
> *position of not really needing any more money. So for the first time,*
> *the bosses aren't in it for profit. If you come and see me and say*
> *'I've had such and such a dream,' I'll say 'Here's so much money.*
> *Go away and do it.' We've already bought all our dreams.*[47]

Without Epstein to guide them, the Beatles decided that they could manage the venture themselves. However, the Company quickly became chaotic. They were swamped with applicants for financial support, and many were given money and never seen again. Apple's employees ran up huge bills, spending money on drugs, alcohol, international calls and expensive restaurant meals. The chaos was nicely illustrated by the memo sent to Apple's employees from George Harrison regarding a group of visiting Hell's Angels (who in the end overstayed their welcome and had to be asked politely to leave.) More detail of the incident, including the memo itself, can be seen on the Beatles Bible website.[48]

Eventually, Neil Aspinall, a schoolfriend of McCartney, Harrison and Lennon, was appointed to run the company on a temporary basis. Aspinall had operated as the band's roadie, driver and general *"fixer"* from 1961 onwards. He began by charging each member of the band five shillings (25p) per concert. He made a range of contributions over the years, including suggesting that Sergeant Pepper be a compere who introduced the band; finding photographs of the characters to appear on the album's cover; playing percussion on individual tracks; and singing on the chorus of Yellow Submarine. He also had an affair with Mona Best, mother of the band's original drummer, Pete Best, and owner of the Casbah Coffee Club in Liverpool, where the Beatles frequently played. The affair resulted in the birth of a son: Vincent "Roag" Best. Aspinall objected unsuccessfully when Pete Best was sacked as drummer by Brian Epstein, and his affair with Mona Best ended shortly afterwards.

In 1969, Allen Klein took over at Apple. Initially, he dismissed Aspinall, but reinstated him when the band members complained. He then instituted a programme of radical and ruthless cost-cutting, in order to try to enable the Company to recover from its financial chaos. However, he quickly fell out with Paul McCartney. When Apple was set up, the band members had signed an agreement which meant that all their activities went through the Company. McCartney found that the release date of his album was delayed in order to allow the prior release of *Let it Be*. Additionally he disagreed over musical changes made to the *Long and Winding Road*. As a result, McCartney instituted a court case against Klein and other band members, leading to the partnership being dissolved. Klein later fell out with the other band members, and following a series of legal disputes, left with a £3.5m payout in 1977. He was jailed in 1979 for having failed to declare income on the sale of Apple promotional records.

The Company continued to operate even after the Beatles broke up, and is still based in London. In addition to the long-running legal dispute with Klein, Aspinall also led Apple Corps to success in two other legal battles. Following allegations in 1979 that EMI and Capitol Records owed more than £10.5 million in unpaid royalties to the Beatles, an increased royalty rate and improved accounting arrangements were agreed. However, Apple sued EMI again for unpaid royalties in 2005, leading to a confidential settlement in 2007.

In 1987 Apple sued Nike and their advertising agency, and EMI and Capitol Records, following the unauthorised use of the song, *Revolution*, in a Nike commercial. EMI claimed that Yoko Ono had authorized its, on behalf of John Lennon's estate. The case was settled out of court in November 1989, in a confidential settlement, though it was rumoured that a large payment had been made to Apple.

Neil Aspinall remained as Chief Executive Officer until April 2007. He died aged 66, from lung cancer in March 2008. An obituary in the Guardian described him as *"one of the few who enjoyed the Beatles' unquestioned trust, not least because he never attempted to grab a share of their limelight."*[49]

Apple Computer Inc

Apple Computer was established on April 1st, 1976 by Steve Jobs, Steve Wozniak, and Ronald Wayne. It was incorporated nine months later, on January 3rd, 1977 by Jobs and Wozniak. By then Wayne had sold his share of the company to Jobs and Wozniak for $800. Despite suffering a decline between 1986 and 1997, Apple Inc (as it is now known), is now the largest publicly traded company in the world. It reported profits of $41.7 billion in 2011-12, owns 250 retail stores in the USA, and 140 elsewhere in the world, and employs over 75,000 people.

The first Apple product was the Apple I computer. Apple is now famous for a wide range of products including the Mac Computer range; the iPod, iPhone and iPad; and the iTunes Browser and Music Store.

Rumours existed that Steve Jobs chose the name Apple because of his love of the Beatles. Indeed, Neil Aspinall claimed during the 2006 court case that Steve Jobs told him this personally. However, at the same time, an Apple spokesman denied it, stating that the name had been chosen because it came before *Atari* (a major competitor) in the telephone book.

The original Apple logo incorporated a drawing of Isaac Newton sat under a tree. This was replaced within a year by a simpler, more colourful and quirkier logo. An "*urban myth*" suggested that the image of an apple with a bite taken out was a tribute to Alan Turing. Turin was a scientist who worked on code-breaking during the second world war. He also undertook research into artificial intelligence. He is now credited with having created the foundations for modern-day computers, but during his lifetime he was not recognised, and was penalised for his homosexuality. He committed suicide in 1954, apparently by taking a bite from an apple which was laced with cyanide. Rob Janoff was the designer who created Apple Computer's second logo. In an article on the CNN website in 2011, he expressed his pleasure at the story, but observed that there was no truth in it:

> *I'm afraid it didn't have a thing to do with it. [..] It's a wonderful urban legend.*[50]

In 1998, the rainbow logo was replaced with a monochrome logo, which would look better if featured in a larger version on the new products (as well as presumably saving costs). This was altered slightly into the stylised logos now used.

Apple Computer Inc was no stranger to legal disputes, having been involved a broad range of cases since its foundation, covering areas including intellectual property protection; antitrust; unfair trade practices; defamation; consumer claims and corporate espionage.

Conflict between Apple and Apple

The possibility of conflict between the two companies arose in 1978 when George Harrison apparently noticed the Apple logo in a computer magazine, and passed details on to Neil Aspinall. Apple Corps took action against Apple Computer, but it was settled relatively easily, by reported payment of $80,000, and an agreement that Apple Computer would not enter the music business. However, problems resurfaced in 1989, after Apple Computer incorporated an Ensoniq sound chip into the Apple II computer, providing MIDI and audio-recording capabilities. This led to Apple Corps taking court action which resulted in a 100 day trial, before two settlements were agreed: the Settlement Agreement, which was reported to have included arrangements for a payment of $26m from Apple Computer to Apple Corps, and the Trade Mark Agreement, which made provisions for future operations, allowing Apple Computer a wider field of use.

Trade Mark Agreement (TMA)

As part of the settlement of the 1989 court case, Apple Computer paid Apple Corps $26 million. In return, Apple Computer's boundaries were extended to enable them to use their marks in relation to equipment and delivery services for musical content, though not for musical content itself. The laid out specific definitions and boundaries:

Apple Corps' field of use	The record business; the Beatles; Apple Corps' catalogue; artists and all related material.
Apple Computer's field of use	The computer, data processing and telecommunications business

Apple Corps' marks	*(i) any design, reproduction or other depiction of an apple, in whole or in part, except a 'rainbow' or multicolour striped apple (in whole or in part) or any apple (of any color(s)) with a 'bite' removed; and (ii) the words 'Apple', and 'Zapple').*
Apple Computer's marks	*(i) any design, reproduction or other depiction of an apple, in whole or in part, except for a whole green apple or a half apple (of any colour); and (ii) the word 'Apple').*

Paragraph 4.3 of the Trade Mark Agreement was an important section, highlighting some areas of overlap:

The parties acknowledge that certain goods or services within the Apple Computer Field of Use are capable of delivering content within the Apple Corps field of use.

The paragraph then went on to explain how such overlap would be dealt with, by allowing Apple Computer to have exclusive rights to use and control their marks in connection with goods such as software, hardware or broadcasting services used to deliver musical content, whilst excluding use relating to physical media delivering content within Apple Corps' field of use. At first, this allowed the two companies to operate peacefully together, however by late 2003 Apple Computer's products and activities had diversified further, and Apple Corps felt they were in breach of the Trade Mark Agreement. A full timeline of key events in the relationship between Apple Corps and Apple Computer is shown below.

04/12/67	The Beatles Limited changes name to Apple Music Limited.
09/02/68	Apple Music Limited changes name to Apple Corps Limited.
19/03/68	Apple Trademarks registered.
01/04/76	Apple Computer founded by Steve Jobs and Steve Wozniak.
Nov 1981	First agreement made between Apple Computer and Apple Corps regarding use of trademarks. Apple Computer authorised to use Apple logos in relation to computer goods but not computer equipment *"specifically adapted for the use in recording or reproduction of music, or in relation to operational services relating to music"*. Authorisation excluded for use of trademarks relating to *"apparatus specifically designed and intended for synthesising music"* unless certain restrictions were met.
1989	Apple Corps sues Apple Computer for breaking the 1981 agreement. The trial in London lasted 100 days before being settled by a Settlement Agreement and a Trade Mark Agreement. Dispute over the Trade Mark Agreement led to the 2006 court case.
Jan 2001	Apple Computer launched iTunes software as a computerised "jukebox" allowing tracks to be loaded and played back on computers.
Oct 2001	iPod introduced and iTunes used to transfer music from computer to iPod.

31/01/03	Prototype of iTunes demonstrated to Neil Aspinall, CEO of Apple Corps.
Nov 2002 to April 2003	Agreement reached with the top five major record companies (Warner, Universal, EMI, Sony & BMG) to distribute music through iTunes.
Apr 2003	iTunes Music Store launched in the USA. Reached the UK in 2004. Originally accessed via www.applemusic.com highlighting clear link between Apple and iTunes.
29/03/06 to 05/04/06	Apple Corps Limited v Apple Computer Inc in High Court (Chancery Division) London.
08/05/06	Mr Justice Mann announces his judgment.
06/02/07	Settlement announced resolving the dispute between Apple Corps and Apple Computer.
11/04/07	Neil Aspinall leaves Apple Corps.
24/03/08	Neil Aspinall dies.
16/11/10	Beatles music available through iTunes Music Store.
05/10/11	Steve Jobs dies.
24/10/12	Apple Inc granted ownership of Apple Corps logo, one year after filing for it.

The 2006 court case

The court case between Apple Corps Limited (Claimant) and Apple Computer Inc (Defendant) took place in London from 29th to 31st March, and 3rd and 5th April, 2006, before Mr Justice Mann. Apple Corps were represented by Geoffrey Vos. Apple Computer were represented by Lord Grabiner.[51]

The parties had already met in court two years earlier, when Apple Computer applied to move the hearing of the case to California. After a three day hearing the same judge who would eventually hear the full case ruled that the case should be held in England, on the grounds that it would be more disruptive, and cost more in terms of pre-trial preparation, in California.

"Core" of the dispute

Apple Corps considered that the use of the Apple logo in relation to the iTunes Music Store (ITMS) was a breach of the Trade Mark Agreement, as they regarded it as use of the logo in relation to music content. They submitted a list of evidence to support their contention that the logos were used on or in connection with musical content rather than simply in connection with software, hardware or broadcasting services used to deliver musical content. Mr Justice Mann summarised the evidence offered to support this contention in different categories.

Use of the Apple logo within the iTunes Music Store

- The Apple logo appeared on screen when the iTunes Store was accessed, and then reappeared when the connection was made with the Store itself (and with the musical content within the Store.)

Materials promoted and distributed within the iTunes Music Store

- Tracks and collections were offered exclusively through iTunes Music Store for a limited period.

- Some material was recorded exclusively, and distributed exclusively, through iTunes Music Store, although apparently there had been no more than ten such recordings.

- Playlists were promoted featuring the favourite tracks of performing artists.

- Collections of recordings were promoted, sometimes including tracks which had not been released previously.

- Selections of favourite tracks chosen by "iTunes Music Store staff experts" were marketed under the title of "iTunes Essentials."

- Unsigned artists could sign up with iTunes so that their tracks could be promoted alongside other iTunes products.

Video advertisements

- A video entitled *My Generation* was broadcast on TV, promoting the iPod and the iTunes Music Store, and incorporating the Apple logo and the name of AppleMusic.com.

- Three other videos, featuring U2, Coldplay and Eminem, promoting iPod and iTunes Music Store, and incorporating apple logos were also broadcast.

Other promotional initiatives

- Gift cards were produced and were promoted on leaflets which referred to iTunes as being the number one music download stored and "*the best jukebox around*".

- Other advertisements included the Apple logo and made references to the iTunes music store.

- Email circulars were sent to participating account-holders, containing the Apple logo, and promoting recorded music content available through iTunes Music Store.

- A range of other advertising included the words "*applemusic.com*" and the Apple logos.

- Statements from Apple and Steve Jobs regarding Apple's vision and activities.

- A statement in the formal Securities and Exchange Commission Annual Report claimed that the Company was "*integrating the entire end-to-end music solution, including the hardware (iPod), software (iTunes) and music content (iTunes Music Store)*".

- A speech given by Steve Jobs in April 2003 compared Apple Computer's activities in providing legal downloads with the traditional sale of CDs.

Mr Justice Mann's Analysis and Decision

Mr Justice Mann divided his analysis of the case into two areas:

- An evaluation of whether the apple logo was used by Apple Computer on or in connection with recorded music, contrary to the Trade Mark Agreement.

- An appraisal of whether Apple Computer's use of the logo was permissible according to clause 4.3 of the Trade Mark Agreement.

The first step in addressing the above two questions was to analyse the meaning of relevant sections of the Agreement itself. In his summary judgment, Mr Justice Mann commented that the parties were not in agreement about what the TMA actually meant, observing:

Both parties submitted that the position is simple and straightforward, which is a pretty good indication that it is not.

He also highlighted the fact that the Trade Mark Agreement was written in 1991, at a time when technology was in a much less developed state than it was at the time of the trial, without the internet and without widespread data transmission via telephone lines. He emphasised that this should be borne in mind when interpreting the agreement.

The important factor in examining the first question was to clarify the meaning of the phrase *"on in or connection with."* Mr Vos, representing Apple Corps, submitted that the phrase should be interpreted widely, covering *any* use of the trademarks in relation to activities within the field. He maintained that Apple Computer's use of the Apple logo in the iTunes Music Store was an infringement, as it was used on or in connection with musical content as well as in connection with a delivery service. He concluded that Apple Computer was effectively acting as a record company in selling musical content in its original format, and in repackaged formats.

Conversely, Lord Grabiner, representing Apple Corporation, maintained that the phrase referred to *"use which indicates the source or origin of the rights in, or the right to control, the music."* He claimed that Apple Computer would only have infringed the agreement if it had used the trademarks to suggest that the Company was the originator, or rights-owner, of the musical content. However, he declared that Apple Computer only used the logos in relation to products and services within its own field of use (e.g. iPod and the delivery service), and argued that the Company always made it clear who owned the copyright in the music.

To assist in his deliberations, Mr Justice Mann examined the Trade Marks Acts of 1905 and 1938, and the case of *R v Johnstone [2003] 1 WLR 1736* in which Lord Nicholls observed:

> *the essence of a trade mark has always been that it is a badge of origin. It indicates trade source: a connection in the course of trade between the goods and the proprietor of the mark.*

Mr Justice Mann concluded that Mr Vos's interpretation of the phrase "*on or in connection with*" was too wide, but that Lord Grabiner's interpretation was too narrow. He laid down his own interpretation of the phrase as "*a degree of trade connection or association with that subject matter relating to its commercial origin.*"

The second question focused on Clause 4.3 of the Agreement. The full text of Clause 4.3 stated:

> *The parties acknowledge that certain goods and services within the Apple Computer Field of Use are capable of delivering content within the Apple Corps Field of Use. In such case, even though Apple Corps shall have the exclusive right to use or authorize others to use the Apple Corps Marks on or in connection with content within subsection 1.3(i) or (ii), Apple Computers shall have the exclusive right to use or authorize others to use the Apple Computer Marks on or in connection with goods or services within subsection 1.2 (such as software, hardware or broadcasting services) used to reproduce, run, play or otherwise deliver such content provided it shall not use or authorize others to use the Apple Computer Marks*

*on or in connection with physical media delivering pre-recorded
content within subsection 1.3(i) or (ii) (such as a compact disc of
the Rolling Stones music).*

The clause cross-referenced other subsections of the Agreement.
These subsections defined the *"field of use"* for each of the
Companies:

*1.2 'Apple Computer Field of Use' means (i) electronic goods,
including but not limited to computers, microprocessors and
microprocessor controlled devices, telecommunications equipment,
data processing equipment, ancillary and peripheral equipment, and
computer software of any kind on any medium; (ii) data processing
services, data transmission services, broadcasting services,
telecommunications services; (iii) ancillary services relating to any
of the foregoing, including without limitation, training, education,
maintenance, repair, financing and distribution; (iv) printed matter
relating to any of the foregoing goods or services; and (v)
promotional merchandising relating to the foregoing.*

*1.3 'Apple Corps Field of Use' means (i) the Apple Musical
Artists; the Apple Catalog; personalities or characters which appear
in or are derived from the Apple catalog; the names, likenesses,
voices or musical sounds of the Apple Musical Artists; any musical
works or performances of the Apple Musical Artists; (ii) any
current or future creative work whose principal content is music
and/or musical performances; regardless of the means by which
those works are recorded, or communicated, whether tangible or
intangible; (iii) promotional merchandise relating to any of the
foregoing;*

Mr Vos maintained that the clause confirmed Apple Corps'
exclusive rights to use the Apple trademarks in relation to musical
content, and that it demonstrated that if Apple Computer wished
to use the marks in relation to a service delivering musical

recordings then it needed to ensure that it was clear that the marks had no connection with the musical content.

Mr Justice Mann did not accept Mr Vos's argument. He observed that the clause must have been included in order to cover areas of conflict or confusion, rather than, as Mr Vos appeared to be suggesting, simply re-stating agreement over fields of use which were laid out elsewhere in the Agreement. He broke the clause down into three sentences, and then outlined his interpretation of their meaning:

> *There may be circumstances in which Apple Computer legitimately use their trademarks in association with a system which delivered musical content. In such circumstances, (whilst recognising Apple Corps' rights in this area), Apple Computer can do this without infringing Apple Corps' rights. However, this does not entitle Apple Computer to use their trademarks on or in connection with physical media delivering pre-recorded content within subsection 1.3(i) or (ii)*

Mr Vos attempted to argue that the third part of Clause 4.3, as broken down above, prohibited Apple Computer from using its trademarks in relation to the sale of musical content through the iTunes Music Store. He supported this by referring to subsection 1.3 (ii), which included within the definition of Apple Corps' field of use the phrase *"regardless of the means by which those works are recorded, or communicated, whether tangible or intangible."* He concurred with Steve Jobs' statement that downloads were simply the next step on from CDs, and maintained that *"any reasonable person"* would see a permanent download as *"physical media."*

Mr Justice Mann did not accept this argument. He observed that it would be

> *a serious distortion of fairly plain notions to say that files delivered by ITMS and stored somehow in digital form, and/or the hard disk*

which stores them, amount to "physical media" which "deliver"
pre-recorded content.

He also dismissed Mr Vos's reference to subsection 1.3 (ii), noting that the word "*intangible*" was not referring to the musical content, but to the means of recording or communication. He concluded by stating:

Provided that the mark is used in a reasonable and fair way on or in
connection with the service, and genuinely (non-colourably) to
denote a trade connection with that service (rather than with
anything else), then the line will not be treated as crossed.

Evaluating the alleged breaches

Having established an explanation of "*on or in connection with*", and clarified clause 4.3, Mr Justice Mann then considered the alleged breaches in the light of those interpretations.

The use of the Apple logo within the iTunes Music Store

The Judge compared the use of the Apple logo by Apple Computer within the iTunes Music Store to the way in which a high street retailer might utilise their own logo within their store, selling goods from other sources, but without any intention to suggest that their own logo was a badge of origin for those goods. He did not accept Mr Vos's contention that the fact that the Apple logo disappeared and then reappeared when the link to the content had been secured meant that an association was being established between the content and the trademarks.

Furthermore he concluded that this form of use of the Apple logo by Apple Computer within the iTunes Music Store was "*precisely the sort of situation that clause 4.3 was intended to address*" and determined that the use was "*genuine (non-colourable), reasonable and fair.*" He was further persuaded by the fact that Apple

Computer made it absolutely clear who owned the rights to the music available through the store, and concluded that the use was not a breach of the Trade Mark Agreement.

Materials promoted and distributed within the iTunes Music Store

In considering the exclusive tracks, the playlists, selections and special recordings, the Judge rejected the view that, in order to determine whether these activities breached the Trade Mark Agreement, he should consider whether or not these demonstrated that Apple Computer were acting as a record company. Again, he compared the situation to a high street retailer who might make in-store offers, or re-package items. He did accept that the *"special recordings"* were the most contentious of the offerings, but still believed that the use of the apple logos was limited to the data transmission service, and therefore acceptable within the agreement, particularly in the light of his interpretation of clause 4.3.

Video advertisements

The Judge agreed that Apple Computer's logos appeared in the four video adverts, all of which promoted the availability of recorded music. However, his view was that the use of the logos and the *"dramatic music and visual presentations"* were aimed at promoting the availability of music in the iTunes Music Store, rather than promoting the specific music being used within the advertisements. He did not see the logo use as suggesting an association with the works themselves, and in any event believed that it had not crossed the line laid down in clause 4.3 of the Trade Mark Agreement.

Other promotional initiatives

Mr Justice Mann considered a sample of advertisements, and the email advertising, and concluded that the Apple Computer marks were again used in an acceptable manner, which was associated with the download service, and not the musical content itself.

Statements from Apple and Steve Jobs regarding Apple's vision and activities

Mr Justice Mann also examined submissions from Mr Vos that the claims made by Steve Jobs and Apple Computer that they were offering a *"seamlessly integrated solution"* for consumers meant that they were breaching the Trade Mark Agreement by using their marks in connection with musical content. However, he dismissed the submission, putting it down as *"marketing-speak"*, and suggesting that it bore no importance compared to what they *actually* did with their logos, and how a *"reasonable user"* would interpret those actions.

Epilogue

As a result of the above, Mr Justice Mann concluded that Apple Computer had not breached the Trade mark Agreement. He also ruled that Apple Corps would pay Apple Computer's legal costs, estimated at $2m, though he rejected a request for an interim payment of $1.5m.

In reacting to the judgment, Neil Aspinall commented *"With great respect to the trial judge, we consider he has reached the wrong conclusion"*.[52] He confirmed that they still believed that Apple Computer had broken the agreement, and affirmed that they would be taking the case to the Court of Appeal. However, this never happened. Instead, an agreement was reached between the two companies in 2007, resulting in Apple Computer purchasing the trademarks, and then licensing some of them back to Apple Corps for their continued use.

Steve Jobs, the CEO of Apple Inc., commented

We love The Beatles, and it has been painful being at odds with them over these trademarks[...] It feels great to resolve this in a positive manner, and in a way that should remove the potential of further disagreements in the future.[53]

Neil Aspinall also added his pleasure at the agreement:

It is great to put this dispute behind us and move on. The years ahead are going to be very exciting times for us. We wish Apple Inc. every success and look forward to many years of peaceful co-operation with them.[54]

Sadly, Aspinall died the following year, and Steve Jobs died in October 2011. Following Jobs' death, an unauthorised modification to Apple Computer's logo quickly spread round the world. There was dispute over who had created it, with it being widely attributed to Jonathan Mak Long, a design student from Hong Kong. However, a UK-based graphic artist Chris Thornley, claimed to have created it several months earlier, and a Los Angeles resident Farzin Adeli also claimed the design. Mak and Thornely accepted that they had individually come up with the same idea. Thornley sold the design on his website,[55] to raise money for cancer charity. Adeli filed for copyright, and also sold the design for a cancer charity, however it was suggested that any copyright claim would be opposed either by Apple, or by Steve Jobs' estate. Mak was later contracted to design an advert for Coca Cola.

The tribute mirrored a gesture from Jobs himself who, despite the legal wrangles between the companies, arranged for a tribute to be placed on Apple Computer's homepage in 2001, following the death of George Harrison.

The case of Apple vs Apple was notable not only because two iconic, worldwide companies, which emerged from the hippy culture of the 60s and 70s, ended up spending a fortune in court arguing over a pictorial representation of a fruit. The judgment highlighted that two similar trademarks can work alongside each other in different sections within the same industry. The trademark system is intended to restrict marks to the areas for which they are registered, and Mr Justice Mann appeared to make a judgment which was consistent with that. He appeared to believe that consumers are not easily confused or misled and, in the same way that they could differentiate between a physical store and the goods within it, could distinguish between the trademark relating to iTunes Music Store, as an *"electronic shop"*, and the goods on sale within that electronic shop.

Overall, Apple Corps probably benefited most financially out of the whole affair. In *"Many Years from Now"*, a biography of Paul McCartney, by Barry Miles, McCartney is quoted as commenting:

> *actually the fact that we copyrighted (sic) the name Apple is one of the things that has made us the most amount of money.*

It should be said that this was before they lost the 2006 case, nevertheless, the $26m agreement in 1991, and the sale of the logo to Apple Inc in 2007, will certainly have contributed substantial funds to Apple Computer.

CONFIDENTIAL INFORMATION

THE GREAT TICKET SCANDAL

Viagogo

Viagogo Limited describes itself as an online exchange service. Established in 2006, it now has websites in over 25 countries. It promotes itself as a location where fans can buy and sell tickets for live events, enjoying a range of benefits:[56]

- Security - avoiding the dangers of buying potentially forged tickets from street touts.

- Access - giving fans the chance to get highly sought-after tickets.

- Price transparency - all prices clearly listed on the website and "set" by the market.

- Privacy - a guarantee that customers' transactions are private and protected.

The secondary ticketing market has been subject to criticism for some time. In January 2011, MP Sharon Hodgson brought the Sale of Tickets (Sporting and Cultural Events) Bill before Parliament for its Second Reading. The Bill aimed to allow event organisers and promoters to prevent tickets being resold by unauthorised retailers for more than 10% above the ticket's face value. The bill was talked out of time by Conservative MPs. Despite this, in the court case examined here Viagogo referred to a letter from the Minister for Employment Relations Consumer and Postal Affairs which appear to support their business model:

the government has no problem with the principle of a secondary market for the resale of tickets. An honest and well-functioning secondary market provides valuable services for consumers, both those who have surplus tickets because their plans change, and those who are prepared to pay higher prices for last minute availability [...] However, the government does deplore the activities of fraudulent ticketing websites ... We therefore welcome the practices of websites, such as Viagogo, who are offering genuine fans a forum in which to sell their tickets to other fans.[57]

Hardcash Productions

Hardcash Productions was set up in 1992 by David Henshaw, initially to remake an undercover documentary about tight-fisted employers which was originally made for the BBC, but not transmitted for legal reasons. The documentary was sold to Channel 4 under the name *"Undercover"* and the company name was a reference to that initial production. The Company produced a wide range of high profile, and often controversial documentary and current affairs programmes for Channel 4 and the BBC, winning a series of awards including three Emmys, three RTS Journalism awards, a Bafta, and a Grierson documentary award.

The Great Ticket Scandal was produced in February 2012 to research the world of online ticket reselling, to investigate where tickets on secondary ticket websites come from, and to examine why such websites are able to offer substantial numbers of tickets within minutes of the official box offices opening and/or selling out. The programme was produced for Channel Four's Dispatches series, and focused on two companies in particular: Viagogo Limited and Seatwave. It gathered evidence using undercover reporters working for the two companies. The programme was scheduled for broadcast on 23 February 2012.

On 7th February Hardcash Productions sent a letter (by fax, email and post), to Viagogo Limited, to advise them that an individual named Paul Myles, who had been employed by them from 28th November 2011 until 13th January 2012, had been undertaking covert filming during his employment. The letter further advised them that evidence would be presented in the documentary to demonstrate that their presentation of the company as an online ticket exchange for fans was *"not entirely accurate."* They stated that:

> *Our evidence shows that your model often operates to ensure that tens of thousands of tickets are not being sold to the public through primary outlets and then re-sold, but are initially being offered for sale to the general public through Viagogo. These tickets are received by you as allocations from promoters.*

The letter included an extract from the script, in which Mr Myles was warned by a manager at Viagogo to keep quiet about the allocations which Viagogo received from promoters:

> *It is really important that we never communicate to anyone, either buyer or sellers, that these accounts exist and that we do have tickets, because that is something internal that they are not supposed to know.*

Viagogo's response to the letter came via their solicitors, Lewis Silkin, who requested evidence that Hardcash had complied with the Ofcom code and Channel 4's protocols when obtaining the evidence. They promised a further, more comprehensive response by the end of Friday 17th February.

This further response was actually sent on 20th February. It stated that an injunction would be sought on 21st February, unless Hardcash Productions and Channel 4 had undertaken by 4.30 p.m. on 20th February, not to *"broadcast, disclose or otherwise communicate certain confidential information."*

No such undertaking was provided by Hardcash or Channel 4, and as a result, Viagogo Limited made an application for urgent injunctive relief against Paul Myles; Hardcash Productions Limited; and Channel Four Corporation Limited. The case was heard in the England and Wales High Court (Chancery Division) by Mr Justice Hildyard on the 22nd February; a detailed judgment was provided the following day.

Injunction

An injunction has been defined as:

> *A court order by which an individual is required to perform, or is restrained from performing, a particular act [...] It is an extraordinary remedy, reserved for special circumstances in which the temporary preservation of the status quo is necessary [...] An injunction is usually issued only in cases where irreparable injury to the rights of an individual would result otherwise.*[58]

An injunction may be permanent or temporary, and may be withdrawn by the court at a later stage.

Viagogo's application

Viagogo were keen to highlight that their application was not trying to halt the programme altogether, but was limited to preventing the disclosure of the confidential information gained by Mr Myles during his employment:

> *We make it clear at the outset that our client will not be seeking to restrain by injunction the publication of any defamatory allegations against it and nor does it seek to restrain the broadcast of any general statements about its business. The points you wish to make about our client can be made without the disclosure of its confidential information.*

They recognised that remedies were available to them in other respects, either by suing Hardcash for defamation, or by complaining to Ofcom. They also attempted to address any argument that might be put forward that there was a public interest justification for Hardcash obtaining the confidential information by undercover means. Their lawyers' letter emphasised that their business model had been examined and "*approved*" by the government:

> *the issues that you are raising in the programme are effectively those considered not once but twice by the government which has concluded that the business methodology that you propose to criticise in the Programme is both legitimate and should not be subject to further regulation.*

The letter went on to pre-empt the case which they believed would be put against Viagogo in the documentary:

> *The central criticism which you appear to be levelling at our client is that it is misleading consumers in stating that it is a secondary ticket exchange and not a primary seller. It is, we suggest, abundantly clear that our client does not intend to mislead anyone in this respect. A cursory examination of our client's website reveals that it does sometimes offer primary tickets for sale in partnership with live event promoters and has taken steps to publicise that fact.*

They further suggested that any such criticism could, in any event, be put forward without use of the confidential information, and continued by considering the question of the "*right of free expression guaranteed by Article 10.1 of the ECHR*" (European Convention on Human Rights) citing an observation from the case of *Barclays Bank Plc v. Guardian News and Media Ltd. [2009]*:

> *Freedom of speech is a previous value in a democratic society that the courts must strive to protect and promote. However, that does*

not mean that journalists should have complete freedom to publish in full confidential documents leaked in breach of a fiduciary duty.[59]

They then went on to suggest that revealing the *"highly commercially sensitive"* confidential information would lead to Viagogo losing business from key business partners, with *"very serious consequences to Viagogo's business, its employees, shareholders etc."*

Finally, the lawyers' letter claimed that Mr Myles' actions were a criminal breach of the *Computer Misuse Act 1990*. They expanded this in later statements to the court to suggest that information was obtained by examining accounts within Viagogo's computer systems, and gathering information which would not have been available to him as a customer service associate.

Mr Justice Hildyard's Analysis and Judgment

In undertaking his analysis Mr Justice Hildyard made reference to *Section 12(3) of the Human Rights Act 1998* (which implements the European Convention on Human Rights in the UK). The act, aimed to protect freedom of expression, imposes a high burden on a court, preventing it from stopping publication of material prior to a trial, unless it believes that it is likely that a trial would enable the applicant to prevent publication. The Judge referred to the case of *Cream Holdings v Banerjee [2004] UKHL 44*, which reached the House of Lords, for clarification about how one might determine whether an application was *"likely"* to succeed:

the court is not to make an interim restraint order unless satisfied the applicant's prospects of success at the trial are sufficiently favourable to justify such an order being made in the particular circumstances of the case. As to what degree of likelihood makes the prospects of success 'sufficiently favourable', the general approach should be that courts will be exceedingly slow to make interim

restraint orders where the applicant has not satisfied the court he
will probably ('more likely than not') succeed at the trial.

He went on to highlight *Section 12(4)* which specifically refers to
"journalistic, literary or artistic material" where it would be in the
public interest for it to be published referring to several other
cases and judicial comments which further emphasised the need
for caution when considering applications to prevent publication,
and ending with the comment made by Mr Justice Eady in *CC v
ABB [2006] EWHC*:

*it is clear that prior restraints are viewed as pernicious and that, to
be upheld as justifiable, their use will have to be viewed as
appropriate, proportionate and absolutely necessary.*

Having established that Viagogo would have to satisfy a high
burden of proof in order to win their case, the Judge then
examined the validity of their claim to have a right to protect the
confidential information which Mr Myles acquired during his
employment with them. He defined three steps which need to be
undertaken to achieve this:

- Establish what information exactly it is that they believe is
  confidential.

- Show that there is no reason why this confidentiality should
  be removed from this information.

- Demonstrate that their private right of confidence in the
  information outweighs any public interest reasons for it to
  be disclosed.

Having identified these three steps, the Judge then analysed them
each in turn, using evidence from Viagogo's lawyers' letter of 20th
February and witness statements provided to him.

1. The Confidential Information

A schedule of the alleged confidential information was included within the letter of the 20th February, categorising it in three areas:

- Details of how primary tickets would be sold through the Viagogo website, including the names of promoters and others who had allocated the tickets to Viagogo.

- The number of primary tickets allocated, and the individual and total sale proceeds from these.

- The profit share arrangements between Viagogo and the various suppliers of primary tickets.

The Judge noted that the main parties at risk from disclosure of the confidential information in the first two categories above were the promoters and others who had provided Viagogo with the tickets. This view was supported by Mr Martin Howard, QC, Viagogo's representative who described this part of the claim as:

in effective being derivative, the claimant perceiving it to be its duty to vindicate the rights of the promoters.

Having determined that it was the promoters and other allocators of tickets who were at risk in relation to the first two categories, Mr Justice Hildyard then searched for evidence which might suggest that they were concerned that the information might be published, or which indicated that confidentiality had been promised to them. He made three main comments:

- All those who had passed primary tickets on to Viagogo had been notified about the proposed programme, but only one had responded, and they appeared to have no problem about their relationship with Viagogo being made public.

- No documentation or evidence was provided to prove that the other parties expected Viagogo to keep details of their relationship confidential.

- The Concert Promoters Association, who represented many of the above parties, had issued a statement which suggested they had no problem with it being public knowledge that promoters were distributing tickets through sites such as Viagogo.

He observed that the evidence collected by Mr Myles suggested that it was Viagogo's managers who considered it *"highly unethical"* that the company obtained tickets directly from promoters, and through purchasing them through Ticketmaster. He illustrated this perspective with a quote from the witness statement of David Henshaw, Managing Director of Hardcash Productions:

On the admission of their own managers, the reasons for secrecy are to keep the public in the dark, not for fear of confidential information falling into commercial rivals' hands and that [sic] these activities are, in their managers' own words, 'shady' and 'highly, highly immoral.'

Mr Justice Hildyard then examined the third category of information: the profit share arrangements. He accepted that these *were* relevant to Viagogo's interests, and observed that he was *"more inclined to accept this category should be protected."* However, he noted that inclination would need to be considered in the light of the defendants' claim that such information related to *"improper trading practices."*

2. Why should the information be kept confidential?

Viagogo's case for maintaining the information confidential related mainly to the manner in which the information was obtained. The reporter, who obtained the information, Mr Myles, signed a contract of employment with Viagogo. The contract included a clause which stated:

You will not ... use for your own purposes or disclose to any third party and shall use your best endeavours to prevent the publication or disclosure of any confidential information.

Mr Justice Hildyard acknowledged the importance of this express contractual obligation. In addition, he considered Viagogo's objections to the fact that Myles had been employed as a customer service associate, yet had managed to acquire information which would not have been readily available to him in that role, presumably by abusing his access to the organisation and their computer systems.

The Judge accepted that damage might be done to the organisation if the confidential information were broadcast; however he tempered this by speculating that, certainly in relation to the first two categories of information, some of that damage had been done anyway, as, in line with their protocols, Channel 4 had already informed the promoters and distributors of primary tickets that they were aware of their relationship with Viagogo.

As a result he concluded that only the third category of confidential information justified court protection against disclosure, assuming that public interest reasons did not outweigh such justification.

3.   Private right of confidence versus public interest reasons

In this respect, the Judge ruled fairly strongly in favour of the public interest side of the argument, observing *"there is real substance in the point made by the defendants that the claimant is concealing from the public that its website is used for a substantial amount of primary ticket sales."* He went on to agree with a statement made by the Managing Director of Hardcash Productions that Viagogo's true aim was:

> to prevent members of the public finding out (1) the true source of many tickets; and (2) the extent of Viagogo's collusion with promoters and professional sellers so that they benefit from a huge mark-up on tickets which were never available for sale at face value to the public.

To support this decision he highlighted a range of observations made on Viagogo's website, in statements to the Competition Commission, and in an interview with the BBC, all of which misleadingly claimed that Viagogo was a secondary, fan-to-fan ticket exchange, not a primary seller. He cited several precedents which confirmed that a well-established principle that the media *could* claim to be operating in the public interest by publishing confidential information in order to highlight misleading statements made by an individual or organisation, including Mr Justice Eady, in *McKennit v Ash*:

> where a claimant has deliberately sought to mislead the public on a significant issue, that would be regarded as a sufficient reason for putting the record straight, even if it involved a breach of confidence or an infringement of privacy.[60]

He accepted that there was some evidence on the website and elsewhere that Viagogo was not simply a secondary ticket-seller, however he did not see this as relevant, commenting:

> the overall impression that it creates and which I would expect the public to rely on, is that it is a market for fan-to-fan exchange and not a surreptitious outlet for primary tickets which they would expect to be available at the advertised prices at the box office.

Before concluding, Mr Justice Hildyard mentioned three other considerations.

First, he questioned whether the court was correct in allowing latitude to the producers of the programme to include the confidential information. He concluded that the judgment over whether the material was essential to the case being presented in the programme was one which should be made by the editor.

Secondly, he considered what impact the manner in which the confidential information had been acquired should have on his decision-making. He acknowledged that it was in the public interest to discourage covert gathering of evidence. However, he also recognised that Channel 4 and Ofcom guidelines had been carefully observed by the programme makers, and furthermore, felt that the covert activity was partially justified because of the nature of Viagogo's activities:

> *In any event, as it seems to me, and especially having regard to the view within the claimant itself that the way in which it is conducting its website in this particular respect in relation to primary tickets and the sweeping up of a considerable number of tickets from Ticketmaster, is, to put it no higher, shady.*

Finally, he addressed the suggestion from David Henshaw, that it was too late to withdraw the confidential information from the programme before broadcast, because the material "... *is threaded throughout the Programme and would necessitate complex editing which would take several days.*"

In considering this, he questioned why the case was being examined at a point when any decision to accept the application would cause real difficulties to the broadcaster and programme-maker. However, he did not feel that it was reasonable to blame them for the application being made so late, noting that:

- Detailed information was given to Viagogo on 7 February by Channel 4 and Hardcash Productions of the potentially contentious areas of the programme.

- It took Viagogo some time to respond fully, and it was only on Monday 20th February that they confirmed that they would be applying for an injunction.

As a result of the above, the Judge declined the application, and ordered that the Viagogo should pay their own costs, and those of Channel 4 and Hardcash.

Epilogue and Conclusion

Following the decision, Viagogo made an appeal in the Court of Appeal, just a few hours before the programme was due to be broadcast. The Master of the Rolls, Lord Neuberger, concluded that Mr Justice Hildyard's had considered the matter with care and made a justifiable decision. He emphasised that Viagogo had not acted quickly enough to bring the application.

The programme went ahead as scheduled. The evidence which was presented appeared to show that substantial numbers of tickets for popular events were passed by promoters to secondary ticket sites such as Viagogo, and sold at prices which were well over face value. The additional revenue from these tickets was split, with the secondary ticket site taking around about 15%, and the balance being paid to the promoter. The information which Viagogo attempted to keep confidential included the fact that they had been allocated almost 50,000 tickets from the primary market for big shows in 2012, including:

- 9,000 tickets for a Coldplay Stadium tour.

- Over 3,000 tickets for Westlife's 2012 tour.

- 2,200 tickets for Rihanna's UK tour.

- 800 tickets for the BBC's Strictly Come Dancing live show.

- 800 tickets for the X Factor live tour.

The Great Ticket Scandal was nominated for a 2012 AIB Award in the Best Domestic Current Affairs category. MP Sharon Hodgson, who had campaigned against the secondary ticket sites, and who was featured in the programme, raised the matter in parliament and attempted to ensure that Culture Secretary, Jeremy Hunt, had the opportunity to view it:

> *I am sure that by now the Minister has seen the recent*
> *"Dispatches" programme "The Great Ticket Scandal". If he and, in*
> *particular, the Secretary of State have not, they can have my DVD*
> *copy. It makes for good watching and I recommend that he watch it.*
> *As he knows, the programme provides the most damning proof yet*
> *that consumers are being ripped off—or at least priced out of*
> *cultural events —on an industrial scale. Will he now please commit*
> *to examining the secondary market again with a view to ensuring*
> *that we put fans first?*[61]

Responding on the Minister's behalf, Hugh Robertson, (Parliamentary Under-Secretary of State for the Department of Media, Culture and Sport) confirmed that an investigation would be carried out by the Office of Fair Trading.

Viagogo wrote to Sharon Hodgson defending their actions and position. However, they also confirmed that they would be making changes to their website to:

> *clarify that we are a marketplace, and that, while the majority of*
> *sellers are individuals selling a small number of tickets, we are not a*
> *marketplace exclusively for 'fans selling to other fans.'*[62]

The case highlighted some key points of importance to those who undertake investigative journalism, and those who might seek to stop publication of what they consider to be confidential information:

- The importance of ensuring that guidelines and protocols are followed carefully when using covert (or possibly unlawful) techniques to gather evidence.

- The desire of courts to allow editorial independence in broadcast and publications.

- The willingness of a court to ignore contractual obligations of confidentiality where public interest requirements outweigh private concerns.

- The way in which the court will look beyond the stated application to the substance behind it when making a decision, as illustrated by one of Mr Justice Hildyard's closing comments.

I am bound to ask myself whether, in truth, [...]the true nub is protection of the claimant's business reputation rather than the promoters' allegedly confidential information.

It is difficult to see what Viagogo hoped to achieve by their court application. They themselves stated that Hardcash had sufficient information without the confidential information they tried to suppress. Their partners (the ticket distributors) were aware of the covert filing but did not seem bothered. The other company featured in the programme, Seatwave, did not take any action to prevent broadcasting. Even if Viagogo had won the case, the fact that they had prevented broadcasting of the material might have led many people to reach the conclusion that the material was more damning and embarrassing than it actually was.

As MP Sharon Hodgson observed:

The fact that Viagogo tried to stop the public from seeing what goes on behind closed doors just goes to show that they know they are behaving badly.

In March 2012, Viagogo were in court again, but this time as defendant in relation to their declared "*core*" business of secondary ticket selling. The Rugby Football Union (RFU) were taking action against them in an attempt to obtain the names and addresses of people who resold tickets to its rugby games via the secondary ticketing website. In common with many sports and entertainment promoters the RFU's terms and conditions precluded reselling of tickets. Unlike most of those promoters, however, the RFU were eager to enforce those conditions, by suing anyone who resold a ticket for breach of contract. To do that they needed the names and address of those who had used Viagogo for that purpose. They no doubt would also see such action as a deterrent for others who might consider profiting from reselling rugby tickets. If the RFU were successful then it would, of course, mean that Viagogo would have to break their promise to give their clients complete privacy.

Mr Justice Tugendhat ordered that Viagogo should pass on the names and addresses to the RFU, dismissing Viagogo's argument that it should not be required to divulge the personal details of its customers because of its duty of confidentiality. He accepted the RFU's argument that it was the only way that they could determine who had breached their ticket terms, and also saw it as justifiable action because Viagogo had assisted in that breach.

Viagogo lost an appeal against the order in November 2012. Following that the RFU commented:

Today's dismissal of Viagogo's final appeal sets an important precedent for the sporting industry that rights holders should retain the ability to control their ticketing policy and pricing. If a seller is found to be listing these tickets on secondary websites they face tough sanctions, including possible court action.[63]

Viagogo saw it differently however. In the same report in the Guardian, their director, Ed Parkinson observed:

While the RFU may have run off with a handful of names from sales that took place several years ago, I can assure you this will not happen again ... Our data protection is now better, so fans may therefore now buy and sell rugby tickets on Viagogo with absolute confidence that their information will be protected in future.

ENDNOTES

[1] Joyce v Morrissey & Others [1989] EWCA 1711

[2] http://www.imdb.com/title/tt0426340/

[3] John McCready/Mojo (2002) http://www.rocksbackpages.com/article.html?ArticleID=8544

[4] Schroeder Music Publishing Company v Macaulay [1974] 1 WLR 1308

[5] Zang Tumb Tuum Records Limited and another v Johnson [1993] EMLR 61 ZTT

[6] Silvertone Records Limited v Mountfield and others; Zomba Music Publishers Limited v Mountfield and Others; [1993] E.M.L.R. 152.

[7] Schroeder Music Publishing Company v Macaulay [1974] 1 WLR 1308

[8] Esso Petroleum v Harpers Garage (Stockport) [1968] AC 269

[9] William Nicholl -v- Shaun Ryder (2000) EMLR 632

[10] http://www.musiclawupdates.com/?p=219

[11] http://www.thefader.com/2009/09/16/andy-rourke-vs-morrissey-the-post-it-controversy-continues/#ixzz25n9YLm8p

[12] Joyce v Morrissey & Others [1989] EWCA 1711

[13] Joyce v Morrissey [1999] EMLR 233

[14] Daily Star, December 12 1996

[15] http://true-to-you.net/morrissey_news_051130_01

[16] http://www.gigwise.com/news/15239/morrissey-id-rather-eat-my-testicles-than-reform-the-smiths

[17] http://blog.peta.org.uk/2013/07/morrissey-vs-gordon-ramsay-in-foie-gras-fracas/

[18] www.legal-dictionary.thefreedictionary.com

[19] Bristol & West Building Society v Mothew [1996] EWCA Civ 533

[20] Robbie Williams appeal case reference

[21] http://www.telegraph.co.uk/news/uknews/1571589/Robbie-Williams-apologises-in-court-to-Take-That-manager.html

[22] http://www.robbiewilliams.pl/en/news24/2007/12/04/nigelmartinsmith/

[23] Creation Records & Others v News Group Newspapers [1997] EWHC 370

[24] Para 290: http://www.publications.parliament.uk/pa/ld200607/ldjudgmt/jd070502/obg-9.htm

[25] http://the1709blog.blogspot.co.uk/2012/01/when-birss-meets-bus-study-in-red-and.html

[26] http://www.walkermorris.co.uk/rolls-royces-and-red-buses

[27] Norowzian v Arks Ltd & Anor (No. 2) [1999] EWCA Civ 3014

[28] Hadley v Kemp [1999] EMLR 589

[29] http://sentric.wordpress.com/2011/02/21/an-idiot%E2%80%99s-guide-for-emerging-artists-to-making-money-from-your-music-publishing-rights/

[30] www.legal-dictionary.thefreedictionary.com

[31] Stuart v Barrett [1994] EMLR 448

[32] http://www.telegraph.co.uk/culture/music/rockandjazzmusic/5054105/Spandau-Ballet-interview.html

[33] http://www.independent.co.uk/news/spandau-face-ruin-after-lost-court-case-1090692.html

[34] http://www.oiprc.ox.ac.uk/papers/Mr%20Justice%20Arnold's%20paper.pdf

[35] http://www.telegraph.co.uk/culture/music/rockandjazzmusic/5054105/Spandau-Ballet-interview.html

[36] http://www.standard.co.uk/goingout/music/gary-kemp-personal-tragedy-revived-spandau-ballet-6780536.html

[37] See for example: http://www.youtube.com/watch?v=wkiJfEBWreI

[38]Spice Girls Limited v Aprilia World Service BV EMLR 478 2000

[39] Spice Girls Limited v Aprilia World Service BV EWCA Civ 15 2002 WL45121

[40] With v O'Flanagan [1936] 1 Ch. 575, 586:

[41]
http://business.bournemouth.ac.uk/news/tv_formats_rights_why_pay_when_you_can_cop
y_for_free.html

[42] Celador Productions v Melville; Boone v ITV Network and Another; Baccini v Celader
Productions Limited and Others [2004] EWHC 2362

[43] http://www.independent.co.uk/news/people/profiles/three-wise-men--a-star-and-a-
miracle-743157.html

[44] http://www.c21media.net/archives/19289

[45] http://www.bectu.org.uk/advice-resources/agreements/alliance-for-protection-of-
copyright

[46] http://www.andrewgrahamdixon.com/archive/readArticle/39

[47] http://www.beatlesinterviews.org/db1968.0514pc.beatles.html

[48] http://www.beatlesbible.com/1968/12/04/george-harrison-invites-hells-angels-to-apple/

[49] http://www.guardian.co.uk/music/2008/mar/25/uk.obituaries

[50] http://edition.cnn.com/2011/10/06/opinion/apple-logo/

[51] Apple Corps Limited v. Apple Computer, Inc., [2006] EWHC 996

[52] http://news.bbc.co.uk/1/hi/entertainment/4983796.stm

[53] http://www.apple.com/pr/library/2007/02/05Apple-Inc-and-The-Beatles-Apple-Corps-
Ltd-Enter-into-New-Agreement.html

[54] http://www.law360.com/articles/17927/apple-fab-four-settle-trademark-dispute

[55] http://www.raid71.bigcartel.com/

[56] www.viagogo.co.uk

[57] Viagogo Limited v Paul Myles, Hardcash Productions Limited, and Channel Four Corporation Limited [2012] EWHC 433

[58] www.legal-dictionary.thefreedictionary.com

[59] Barclays Bank Plc v. Guardian News and Media Ltd. [2009] EWHC 591

[60] McKennit v Ash[2008] QB 73

[61]
http://www.publications.parliament.uk/pa/cm201212/cmhansrd/cm120322/debtext/120322-0001.htm

[62] http://www.sharonhodgson.org/great-ticket-scandal-viagogo-responds-to-sharon-hodgson-09032012

[63] http://www.guardian.co.uk/money/2012/nov/21/court-ruling-ticket-resale-websites

Printed in Great Britain
by Amazon.co.uk, Ltd.,
Marston Gate.